The
California
Chaparral
an Elfin Forest

MAP OF CALIFORNIA
CHAPARRAL AREAS

by
W. S. Head

Library of Congress Catalog Card Number—75-24239

ISBN 0-87961-002-6

Cover photo by W. S. Head

2003 Edition

Printed in USA by Mosaic Press.

Naturegraph Publishers has been publishing books on natural history, Native Americans, and outdoor subjects since 1946. Please write for our free catalog.

Books for a better world

Naturegraph Publishers, Inc.
PO Box 1047 • 3543 Indian Creek Rd
Happy Camp, CA 96039
(530) 493-5353
www.naturegraph.com

To My Wife

Grace Ruth Head

Who has so willingly suffered through the many hours I have spent in gathering the following information, which it is hoped will bring happiness and much enjoyment to many who may never have found this strange and wonderful area that is so much a part of this Great State of California.

The photograph on the cover is by W. S. Head.
Other illustrators are listed in Acknowledgements p. 94.

FOREWORD

This is not a guide!

Believe me, when I say this. This is an introductory book for amateurs and the many new residents, who come to enjoy California and another strange and fascinating part of the world of nature.

I have had the pleasure of introducing a number of men, women, and children to the Elfin Forest. Their reactions have been many and varied. Some have expressed amazement that I had the audacity to refer to this area as a forest. They have been quick to point out that there are very few trees; no running streams; very few animals; and few birds. I partly agreed, but then hurriedly reminded them, "That is the superficial appearance."

After a day or weekend in the Elfin Forest, most individuals admit that there is a fascination here. Perhaps not as glaringly apparent as in other forests. In many cases, it was necessary to point out certain sights to them. Within a short time, the newcomers to this country, were asking questions. Then I knew that I had them hooked.

That is the purpose of this book, to hook you! You may have to be a bit more observant; walk a little softer; and crouch a little lower; but what a wonderful, fascinating world you will discover!

TABLE OF CONTENTS

White Back or
Hoary Leaf Ceanothus
Ceanothus crassifolius

RG

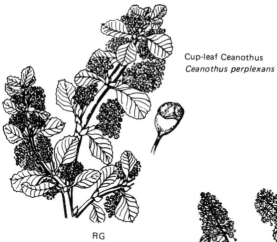

Cup-leaf Ceanothus
Ceanothus perplexans

RG

Woolly Leaved Wild Lilac
Ceanothus tomentosus

RG

CHAPTER 1

CHAPARRAL – WHAT IS IT ?

Chaparral! A name and word colloquial to the southwestern part of the United States.

An easterner would call the vegetation which covers our foot-hills and much of the western slopes of the coast range in Southern California, mere bushes. Similar coverage is found in the southern part of Europe, though not the same species or combination of plants. It is known as "Macchie". Australia has a similar area also, referred to as the "Bush". To the forest ranger as well as the rancher in the United States, it is the watershed. In Mexico, matching areas are called "Chaparro". The early United States settlers in the south-west corrupted the Mexican name to their own fancy—"Chaparral". The name has persisted.

There is a more fanciful and descriptive name to this vast ex-panse of odd foliage. Who first coined the name "The Elfin Forest" I do not know. This name has been used by authors and naturalists over the years. Individuals have applied the name to their ranches.

Elfin Forest seems to be a true English description. It encom-passes the forest and its inhabitants. Most of the bushes are from three to eight feet in height. The wild flowers vary from the "belly type" (you virtually have to lie on the ground to study their grow-ing characteristics) to those that will rise above the four foot level and poke their blooms up through the bush to see the sun.

The Elfin bushes and plants, are not the only small-sized life. There are many animals and birds of Lilliputian size, who have adopted this low forest as their regular residence.

When you gaze out over a hillside covered with this golden and emerald forest, everything appears peaceful and serene. Don't be fooled! In this wilderness the same violence and cold-blooded acts of quick death prevail. Over this Mother Nature dominates; "the survival of the fittest".* It may appear cruel, but actually it is

*Survival by adaptation to the changing conditions of the food supply.

the balancer of life, maintaining equilibrium among species. This keeps one animal, bird, reptile or insect from dominating.

Naturalists and scientists try to understand and study this balance under the name of ecology. To present a very simple explanation, but certainly far from complete, it involves a sort of cycle. The soil depends upon rocks disintegrating along with a goodly amount of dead plants and leaves. The plants depend upon sun, water, and food from the soil for their growth. Many insects depend upon the flowers and foliage for their food; and in turn the birds depend considerably upon the insects for their food. Many small animals depend upon birds for their source of food, while herbivorous animals (cattle, etc.) depend greatly upon the grasses for their food; as man depends partly upon cattle for his food. Man then returns much of the waste to the soil.

It was around the early 1800's that scientists realized that the name biology covered much too much in its scope, so they started dividing the subject up into other subheadings, one of which was ecology. That was over 150 years ago. Like all well-established ways of thought, results are slow to show.

Long before ecology was thought of the Elfin Forest was involved in keeping life going, by providing for all life in its realm. It is a boon for southwestern residents. The vast root system of plants as well as their continuous dropping of surplus foliage, plus the decomposed granite (like large grains of sand) all help make useful soil. When the rains come, and they do at times, the leaves, branches and twigs on the bushes and trees break up the raindrops and scatter the finer drops on the soil. The covering of dropped leaves act as a sponge, and hold much of the water so the roots can have a drink and prevents the water coursing down the sides of the hills. This serves another purpose in that it holds back the water that would cause floods. The water also hastens the decay of the gathered plant particles and thus helps create new soil. Ecology working!

If however, the arch enemy of the Elfin Forest, the BRUSH FIRE, has invaded the chaparral, all of the benefits are lost. Instead the Elfin Forest becomes a destructive menace to the homes built into hillsides. A fire will roar up canyons, burning these expensive hillside homes to the ground. When the rains come, still another menace to those that have been saved from the flames, MUD FLOODS. Without the holding properties of the chaparral and its retentive coverage, the water seeps down into the decomposed granite mixed with newly formed soil. When sufficient water has been absorbed, it starts slowly down the hillside. Like the relentless flow of lava, the mud mixture gathers speed with the aid of additional rain and more mud, until it reaches a home. There seems no protection against it. It seeps under the foundation and comes into the rooms through the floors, pushing in doors, smashing windows and ruining most of the house. Even brick reinforced walls have fallen to this awful flood.

In contrast, below the border in Baja and Mexico, the farmers or herdsmen often deliberately set fire to the Chaparral. They have good reason. First, much of that area is sparcely populated and there is little danger of the fire doing damage. Secondly, it does clear the land rapidly, and in many cases provides additional forage for their cattle as well as providing excellent virgin soil to be easily cultivated. However, our Department of Forestry gets rather jittery about this deliberate burning. When the winds suddenly come from the proper direction, the fire heads for the border with a threat to our Chaparral. Then our fire fighters must swing into action, clearing fire breaks, and taking other preventive measures to stop the onrush of the fire into our more densely populated areas. In my memory, I cannot recall when such a fire has done too much damage to this side of the border, maybe because of our fine fire fighters quick action and good judgement.

There are some seeds in the Chaparral that require the heat of an open flame to crack or in some way effect the coating of the seed or pod, so that the seed will germinate with the coming of the next rain. One of these plants that awaits the flame is the Padre's Staff. *(Oenothera leptocarpa)*. The only time I have found these long slender plants, looking almost like grass, and bearing bright yellow flowers and few leaves, has been in the path of a fire of the year before.

An amazing thing about the plants and shrubs in the Elfin Forest, which have suffered through a fire, is their quick revival. Since these brush fires move rapidly, the root systems are seldom damaged too much. With the water that these roots have stored up, within a few short months, they will start to send out new growth. On one occasion I walked through an area that had been burned over only six weeks before and I was amazed to see new shoots already sprouting out of the rather large ball-like root (burl) of a Chamise. However, to regain full growth does take several years.

There is an interesting story about the far Western Indians and certain burned shrubbery. Often times the heavier trunks of the Manzanita and Chamise are not completely burned and remain standing, still attached to the sturdy burl. As the new growth starts upward, it often will adhere to the dead wood. As the growth proceeds it will wrap its new growth around the old wood leaving a portion of the old wood showing.

It was perhaps some wise old Indian Chief or Medicine Man that observed this phenomenon and the idea of reincarnation was conceived. With a proper introduction to his native followers, he convinced them of the reincarnation, and professed that it was true of humans also. For many years, as the story goes, the Indians held these few revived shrubs in reverence and often worshipped the bushes as loved ones, who had passed away, with the hope that the same phenomenon would happen to their departed one.

A person gradually becomes acquainted with the Elfin Forest and learns through observation and a little study the many things about this fascinating little world. Each day he spends in this forest he will make new friends and be able to call them by name. He will be treated to the discovery of beautiful flowers; become familiar with the birds and their habits; and learn to know the animals, the insects, and the reptiles. If he is lucky and sharp eyed he will witness battles to the death, or the ferociousness of a female protecting her young. He will hear the winds in the trees; and see the beauty of the sunrises and the sunsets. He will witness the violence of a thunder storm that comes from the alabaster white towers of cumulous clouds that rise from the desert into the blue sky.

He will learn the aroma of the perfumed clean air, that follows the summer storm. He will see the sudden transformation of a sky spitting flashes of lightning and vibrating with the thunder clap; then will come the calm, the rain and its clouds will drift into nothingness. The birds will again venture out into the sun, even with the trees still dripping, a time when they sing with unusual joy.

He will have been very close to God and His ways.

RG *

CHAPTER 2

THE PULSE OF LIVING GROWTH

Why does such a forest grow? Why are there more bushes than trees? Why are they all stunted?

There is no one factor, but a combination of several reasons, and most of them are involved with the weather. First, the area covered by this Elfin Forest is considered as a semi-desert. The seasonal changes are very radical, and are not conducive to the requirements of trees. The Chaparral belt is subject to very short rainy periods, with most of the weather year being arid. Such conditions can only support the limited life which exists.

Temperatures during these arid spells and in the dry periods of fall and winter will fluctuate as much as 50-60°, from a low, usually in the 20s or 30s at night, up into the 100s at 2:00 PM in the afternoon. With such conditions the foliage is made tinder dry; ideal for a brush fire. With many of the canyons and slopes facing the west and southwest, from which direction the prevailing winds blow much of the day, at a rate of 3 to 30 miles an hour, the fighting of such fires is made most difficult, because the flames are headed on an up-hill grade. With the prevailing winds fanning the blaze, the fire often travels at a tremendous rate of speed.

As to rainfall when it does fall, for some reason it often seems to skip over the area, with only a drizzle for the Elfin Forest. This is another reason for the promotion of stunted Chaparral growth.

One more cause of this stunting process is the humus-poor soil in which the bushes and plants try to eke out an existence. On most of the hillsides and other areas, besides the canyons, the top and sub-soil usually consists of decomposed granite. Such soil holds very little organic food for plant roots.

The decomposed granite is the result of centuries of disintegration of boulders and stratas of granite. At this stage of break-down, it looks very much like a light brown coarse sand. The crumbling process has been caused by solar heat and frost. Heat expands the

* Mexican Manzanita   *Arctostaphylos pungens* (no basal burl)

particles while the cold frost will cause the grains to contract. Wind then contributes its erosive action by tumbling the grains along the surface of the ground. (Saltation action). Gradually this sand will be infused with organic particles from the flora, and in the next one hundred centuries more or less, the soil will be reduced to a sandy loam.   However, before the soil can become sandy loam the rain leaches out minerals from the decomposed granite because it has little if any absorption properties to hold water.   Instead of holding the water, it quickly lets the water seep through its loose composition into the lower levels, and mineral particles with it.   It is seldom that puddles of water will be seen on the surface of the ground, following a good rain; they have already gone to the lower levels.   Thus little water is retained for the root systems of the Chaparral, another reason for the stunted growth.

So with the lack of rainfall high on the list, plus fluctuating temperatures, and soil composition factors, it is easy to understand why these areas form the Elfin Forest.

Chaparral wild flowers will be found mostly where the soil and decomposed humus forms a good sandy loam, usually on the eastern and northern sides of the hills. Most of these wild beauties are rapid growers. They will shoot up out of the soil in a matter of a week or two, when weather is satisfactory. Then when the weather is hot and dry, they will disappear with the same rapidity.

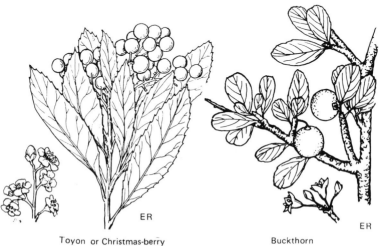

Toyon or Christmas-berry
Heteromeles arbutifolia

Buckthorn
Rhamnus crocea

To include a list of all the bushes and plants which make up the Chaparral is difficult. Several noted botanists have compiled their lists from their findings of the Chaparral that they have explored, but the list proves too long. The list that I present here, with the most approved common names and the scientific or Latin name, is a result of my own findings in the area, covering the Chaparral between the Mexican Border to just south of Los Angeles. The list is set up in order of number or volume of plants and shrubs counted over the given area. In other words Number 1 will be the commonest bush seen, and so on down the list to 12, which is the least common seen.

NUMBER	SCIENTIFIC NAME	COMMON NAME
1.	*Adenostoma fasciculatum*	Greasewood-Chamise (bush)
2.	*Photinia arbutifolia* *Heteromeles arbutifolia*	Christmas-berry — Toyon (bush)
3.	*Rhamnus crocea*	Buckthorn(bush)
4.	*Quercus dumosa*	Scrub Oak (bush to small tree)
5.	*Cercocarpus betuloides*	Mountain-Mahogany (bush to small tree)
6.	*Yucca Whipplei*	Yucca or Our Lord's Candle (stalk with spiny base)
7.	*Fremontia californica*	California Fremontia (bush)
8.	*Prunus ilicifolia*	Holly-leaved Cherry (bush or tree)
9a.	*Ceanothus tomentosus*	Woolly Leaved Wild Lilac (large bush)
9b.	*Ceanothus megacarpus*	Bigpod Ceanothus (bush)
10.	*Arctostaphylos canescens*	Hoary Manzanita (bush or small tree, without basal burl)
11.	*Pickeringia montana*	Chaparral-pea (bush)
12.	*Trichostema lanatum*	Woolly Blue Curls (Med. size bush)

*It will be noted that there are two scientific names given for the Toyon bush. Sometimes scientific names are changed after a botanist (knowledgeable in taxonomy) carefully checks all previous species in that particular group and if he feels that the plant is a new one, the botany taxonomist publishes his findings according to the International Rules of Botanical Nomenclature. Another taxonomist may not agree and may later publish his findings, voiding the first. Often when a name is officially changed, it may take a number of years before the scientific name becomes commonly used by other botanists. Usually, the old name will still be found in unrevised books.

**Here is an example of two common names applying to a single shrub. The scientific name, however, remains the same.

In the *Ceanothus* species, I have set down 7 of the species common to the Chaparral, and most of the species range from Mexico to Los Angeles; *C. leucodermis, C. tomentosus* and *C. perplexans* range farther north; *C. cuneatus* ranges from Oregon south. One species will usually be predominant in an area.

One final note, I should like to make, in regard to these deep southern mountains of California.

For one who travels up and down the state, it has been noted for every thousand feet of elevation traveled in these mountains, you will see a similar flora population 100 miles north, at near sea level. Sometimes I have even noticed a similarity in the topography and the normal weather also. If you traveled to the 3,000 foot level you would observe a similar flora display 300 miles north, near sea level.

The reason this is mentioned is it provides a person an insight into what would be seen if they were planning a vacation to the north. This is not a hard and fast rule, but I have often found that it has helped me.

ER

Mountain-Mahogany
Cercocarpus betuloides

ER

Chaparral-pea
Pickeringia montana

ER

Coffeeberry
Rhamnus californica

The following illustrations are of some other bushes commonly found in the Elfin Forest. Both the common names and the scientific names are given. The common name may change from one area to another but the scientific name is the same the world over.

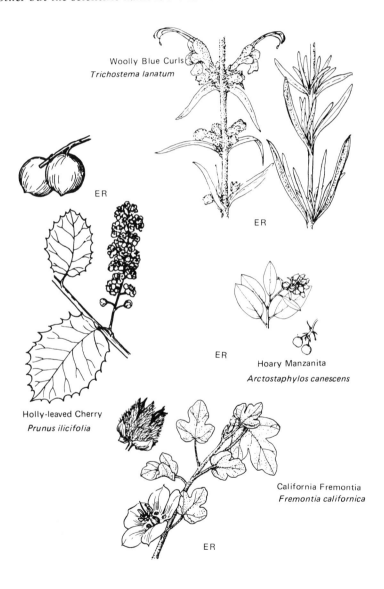

Woolly Blue Curls
Trichostema lanatum

ER

ER

Hoary Manzanita
Arctostaphylos canescens

ER

Holly-leaved Cherry
Prunus ilicifolia

California Fremontia
Fremontia californica

ER

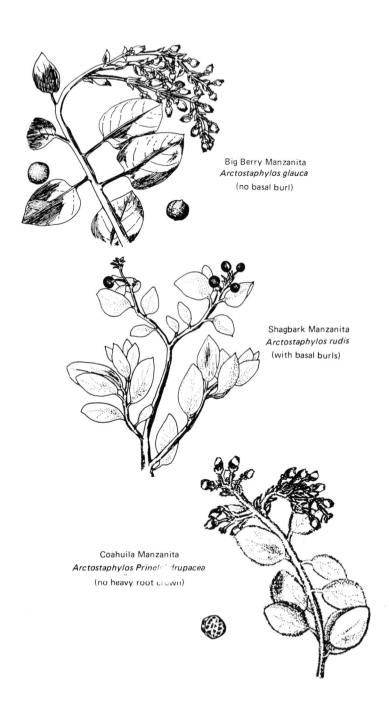

Big Berry Manzanita
Arctostaphylos glauca
(no basal burl)

Shagbark Manzanita
Arctostaphylos rudis
(with basal burls)

Coahuila Manzanita
Arctostaphylos Prinol *drupacea*
(no heavy root crown)

The weather! Ah! The weather!

"Everybody talks about the weather, but nobody does anything about it", wrote the sage, Mark Twain.

There was a good deal said in the last chapter about the effects of the weather on the Elfin Forest, but little was said on how this topsy-turvy weather, creating off-seasons, is brought about.

Nearly all of Southern California often experiences odd weather patterns. Thunder storm rains usually come to the Elfin Forest from the south, southwest, and occasionally from the east, but rarely from the high clouds of the north. The same applies to the winds, with the exception of the east winds without the thunderstorms. These winds come off the Utah and Nevada plateau, and have been dubbed by the residents and the Weather Bureau as the Santa Ana wind.

The southwest winds that prevail over the San Diego area are the results of a north or northwest wind that prevails just off the Southern California Coast. Odd but true.

As a simple explanation, have you ever stood on a small projection of land or a rock in a flowing stream or creek, and watched the current flow past you. As that current of water passed the projection, part of it swirled in behind the rock, forming a rotating or sort of whirlpool of water. This is known as an "eddy", and is what takes place when the off shore prevailing northwest wind blows. It passes Point Loma and starts an eddy of air much larger than in the stream. The wind, is redirected so that it flows in over the city of San Diego and on into the foothills from the southwest. This same action takes place in Los Angeles, after the wind is redirected around Point Firman. Many of the low rain clouds that come down the coast from the Gulf of Alaska are redirected, also.

Usually in October, the Santa Ana season starts in earnest. This is a northwest wind that has its origin in the upper plateaus of Utah

† Indian Manzanita *Arctostaphylos Mewukka* (root-crown or burl)

and Nevada. Very often the Santa Ana follows a storm from the northwest. The first effects of the coming wind are felt in the Santa Ana Canyon, just south of Los Angeles. The wind passes over the hot dry desert and arrives on the west coast mountains and valleys, shooting the mercury up over 100°, and lowering the relative humidity to as low as 3%, and forming very bad fire conditions.

Usually the first gusts of the wind are felt a half hour before sunrise. Then they feel cool, but as the sun rises into the morning sky the wind begins to make its heat felt, in gusts from 10 to 40 or more miles an hour. Trees are uprooted, branches are snapped, and dust and sand blow up in huge clouds.

There has been some controversy on the name of the wind, and how it came about. One theory is that it was named after the famous Mexican General Santa Anna. When he would move his cavalry, they would stir up great clouds of dust that very much looked like those stirred up by the wind. The other version of the name "Santana" comes from and is credited to the mariners. The wind not only makes itself felt on land, but often continues out into the Pacific. Peaceful and calm bays and coves are stirred into a churning mass, sometimes causing ships to drag their anchors. Many navy ships, anchored in San Pedro and San Diego bays, often need to get underway and head out to the open sea to ride out the storm. Thus the mariners using the corrupted Indian name "Santana" which means "Devil wind", coined a good description of a fierce wind.

Since most of these Santa Anas occur in the fall and winter, still another phenomenon takes place, after the wind abates. With the atmosphere clear and bright, the thermometer starts to plummet down until a hard frost settles over the Elfin Forest and the inland valleys. In one day I have seen the temperature go from one hundred degrees to less than thirty degrees; an extreme condition that the Elfin Forest passes through, and helps maintain its stunted type of growth.

Adding another odd feature to this fantastic topsy-turvy land, are the seasons. In most parts of our country the seasons usually follow the position and rotation of the sun. But not the Elfin Forest. When you look at the weather, this is the classification of seasons:

Spring – April, May and June
Summer – July, August and September
Autumn – October and November
Winter – December through March.

Even though this summation has been compiled by a number of weather observers, do not be surprised if there is a variation of a month one way or another. It is possible and it has happened.

To give a brief month by month of what you might expect runs something like this. Please remember that the following, more or less applies, to the Elfin Forest, and not necessarily all of Southern California:

January—
A possible 6 to 7 days of light rain. The average temperature is 65 degrees. A possible low of 32 degrees.

February—
Usually the rainiest month; 2.25 inches is the average rain. The average temperature is 50 to 60 degrees. A possible freeze. Some cloudiness.

March—
The average temperature is 50 to 65 degrees. Some rain in early March. Then an occasional strong wind. Possibly, a few thunderstorms over the eastern Elfin Forest.

April—
A touch of spring. Possibly a few showers (1965 over 5" of rain). The average temperature is 35 to 65 degrees. Sort of a mixed spring and winter.

May—
It is traditionally one of the cloudiest months; usually clearing off before noon. There is seldom more than ¼" of rain. The average temperature is 50 to 75 degrees.

June—
Rainy season is just about over. The average temperature is 40 to 85 degrees. 3 out of 4 days, mornings and evenings, low clouds or fog will cover. Usually clears before noon.

July—
There will be more sunshine and less clouds. It is usually the driest month in the foothills. In the back country the Elfin Forest may have thunderstorms coming up from Mexico, called "Sonoras".

August—

This is the thunderstorm month with more "Sonora Storms". The average temperature is 45 to 100 degrees—plus. Occasional heat waves.

September—

More tropical thunderstorms from Mexico. Usually 1 to 2 heat waves. The average temperature is 50 to 100 degrees—plus.

October—

This is the transition month in the Elfin Forest, from the summer to fall and winter. Possible heat spells. Possible first light rain followed by Santa Ana winds. Much sun. The average temperature is 50 to 100 degrees—plus.

November—

Oddly, this month is considered the one with the ideal weather. It has a few real hot days and some cool nights. Possibly a little rain. Much sunshine. The average temperature is 40 to 90 degrees.

December—

Winter is supposed to start in earnest. However, I have seen the temperature up to 95 degrees on Christmas Day. An average of 6 days rain or drizzle. The average temperature is 60 to 80 degrees. A possible 32 degrees in the Elfin Forest on clear nights.

One final word on the Elfin Forest atmosphere, which can be considered as a part of the weather year. Many times during the year when a person looks towards the foothills they see them nearly obscured by a light gray haze. This effect is mostly on the western slopes of the hills, and is another phenomenon in this small fascinating forest. According to experts the haze is composed of tiny salt particles blown in with an off-shore wind, from the Pacific Ocean some 20 miles to the west of the hills. At times this haze will become very dense, when it becomes mixed with industrial and auto exhaust smoke, a factor, not conducive to good growing conditions for the Elfin Forest.

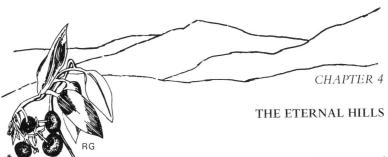

RG

*Many experts have advanced their theories on the formation of Southern California, so an ardent student or amateur soon finds himself at a complete loss, not knowing which theory should be considered as factual. The idea that this area was formed by volcanic action, is soon cast aside by the one who hunts for traces, such as cones, craters, or lava flow and volcanic ash. On the other hand, in 1942 there was an eruption of a new volcano at Paracutin, Mexico, a few hundred miles south of San Diego. This would seem to give the volcanic action theory some credence, but there is still the lack of volcanic traces. The sights that indicate internal pressures are the curvature of the rock stratas on bare hillsides, as well as those that make themselves visible in deep road excavations.

Several theories go along with this internal upheaval idea, which seem to have considerable backing. In my investigations I have seen signs of an alluvial sediment similar to the sediment on the bottom of the sea, at a 300 foot elevation, that was discovered in a cut through a hill for a roadway. This cut was perhaps 2,000 feet long, with the alluvial sediment showing as a huge arc as though it had been pushed up in the middle. Fossils of shells and other shallow sea water life were visible.

The other area appeared like it had once been an ocean beach. The location was near the community of Alpine, California, (about two miles south, and at about 1,500 foot elevation, in very heavy Chaparral). I tried to take specimens, but they were not well preserved and disintegrated when they were picked up. It appeared as though these shells had remained on or near the surface of the soil and had been subjected to considerable erosion. An excavation into this formation might produce samples in better condition.

There are several versions of these upheavals. One is that the land mass rose and sank, twice, from the sea. I am inclined towards this theory because of my two finds mentioned above. Another theory*

*Indian Manzanita *(Arctostaphylos Mewukka)*

sets the upheavals at four. Regardless of the number of times this may have occurred, nearly all experts are in agreement that at some time in the past million years this land mass had been under the sea; that the mighty Colorado River sometimes flowed over the area; and that Southern California was partly the delta of this great river.

I read one account that the huge boulders seen in the many valleys had been washed here by the river. One investigator took samples of these boulders and matched them with the location from which they might have originated. The samples of granite did not match with any local outcroppings. Going on with his theory, he traveled into the southern Rockies and was able to find other granite formations there that matched his specimens from Southern California. If true, and this does sound convincing, you still can take your choice of whatever theory you wish.

There is one interesting observation to be noted on these boulders, regardless from whence they came. It is almost impossible to find one of these boulders completely intact. They are either split apart in one or more places, or they have a cap that has split off from the main body of the boulder. It may seem strange, but this has been caused by the action of frost and solar heat. Cold causes the huge boulders to contract, while the heat of the sun causes the rocks to expand. If this action results in a small split forming, more water will then seep into the crack and as it freezes, it expands with great force, at the same time, causing it to snap off the top, or even split the entire boulder into separate pieces.

If you can find a boulder that has not been affected by this erosion, you will note that it has no sharp angular parts. They are almost always rounded, as though they have spent considerable time tumbling, as in the bed of a river.

An old prospector once told me an interesting story. Old prospectors have vivid imaginations, but I have heard similar stories from others who camp a great deal on the Colorado Desert. Here is his story—

It seems the old boy had made his camp alongside one of these huge boulders that shielded him from a cold night wind out of the Southwest. He rolled up in his blanket and went to sleep. About two or three in the morning he was awakened by a sound, like a rifle shot, and the boulder against which he rested his head gave a sudden jolt.

The old boy built up his camp fire, and took a look at the sur-roundings. He yelled a couple of "Hallos". With no answer, he roll-ed up in his blanket and went back to sleep. In the morning, while he was brewing his coffee, he got to thinking about the noise and the jolt.

Having spent many years camping, the prospector had given the boulder a fairly good going over for possible squirrel holes under the huge rock or even the possibility of a rattlesnake that might disturb him during the night. Now as he gingerly sipped his coffee from a battered tin cup, he started looking the boulder over again. Shortly he came upon a crack, nearly a quarter of an inch wide at the top of the boulder, running from the top and disappearing into the ground at the bottom. He looked carefully and could see inside the crack and noticed that it appeared as a new crack, still unweathered.

Then it dawned on him. The boulder made the noise that had given him the jolt. The night had been cold. Some water probably seeped down in a minute crack, froze, and forced a break in the boulder.

Well, that was the story told by the old prospector, and sometimes they can tell some tall ones. But since that time I have heard other stories from more reliable persons that have more or less confirmed his.

All of this leads up to a partial explanation of the geological be-ginning of the Elfin Forest. Various estimates of the final upheaval range from 10,000 years to half a million or more years ago. The elements have advanced their relentless disintegration of these com-paratively young mountains over eons of time. In a great many parts of the Chaparral belt, (500 to 2,500 foot elevation) much of the surface of the ground appears as decomposed granite, most of which was washed into place after being eroded from a part of the mountains. The denseness of the Chaparral increases constantly, and, with the shedding of its organic parts (leaves and twigs), a stop-ping place for these particles of granite is offered. The further de-composition of the granite and the mixing with organic matter, in many cases has yielded an excellent sandy loam. The coming of the rains will usually wash a portion of this into the canyons and meadows making a fine soil for flowers and grass.

There is little doubt of it, the Elfin Forest does much good, and is one of the binding forces with all that surrounds it.

Buck Brush

Ceanothus cuneatus

ER

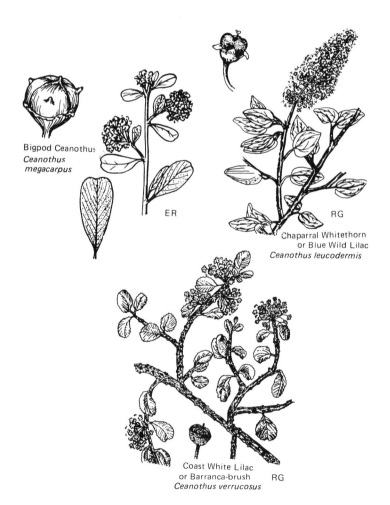

Bigpod Ceanothus
Ceanothus megacarpus

ER

RG

Chaparral Whitethorn
or Blue Wild Lilac
Ceanothus leucodermis

Coast White Lilac
or Barranca-brush   RG
Ceanothus verrucosus

CHAPTER 5

HOW TO EXPLORE THE ELFIN FOREST

To study nature in its natural environs should never become a task, a bore or a requirement. Instead it should be a pleasant adventure, a chance to see those living things that have been created to live in another world set apart from the everyday humdrum of civilized living. It should be a time when man can make friends with both animated and inanimate things; when a man can stroll along a shaded trail on a cool morning, and nod recognition to a colorful Tanager or a scolding Jay bird. There should be a feeling of relaxation among real friends; friends that do not worry about your race or creed, your color or religion.

You should also have that inquisitiveness to know more about your new friends, including their first names, and where they have their residence. You should enjoy their antics, as they try to teach their new born how to fly, hunt, or gather food. You should develop that freeness to look into an azure sky, not filled with towering skyscrapers and smog, but the tops of swaying trees in a soft breeze.

Lastly there should be a certain amount of self satisfaction gained in being able to recognize these creatures of Mother Nature. There is a magic happiness which deeply satisfies a person, brought by being able to point out a delicate Fairy Lantern Lily, *(Calochortus* species) and name it as a friend.

You can go a step further. Try to get the habit of carrying a notebook with you. Make notes; notes about things that do not mean anything at the moment, but later will have more meaning when you have gathered other notes on the same subject. They may be notes of action, location, weather conditions or temperature. Don't worry about the wording or spelling; just so long as you know what you have written. Remember, you don't have to show them to anyone!

When you have reached that stage where you can name a few of your new friends along the trail, to your son, daughter, wife or friend, that will be still more satisfaction!

Yes, you have reached a state of—

"The joy of accomplishment"!

The following are selected notes taken from my own notebooks of observations and studies made over the past ten years. I have tried to write about sights that you are almost surely to come in contact with, any place in the Elfin Forest on your very first visit. I have tried to provide, up to date lists of the various plants and animals you may expect to see as you advance in your observations and studies.

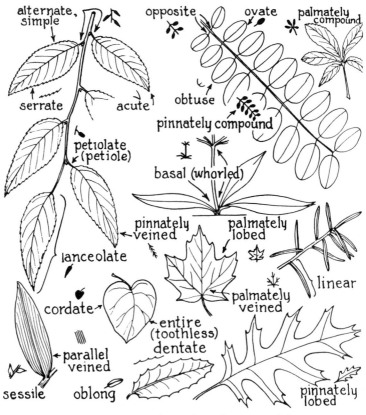

Main types of simple and compound leaves.

Taken from The Amateur Naturalist Handbook by Vinson Brown, artist Donald Kelley, by permission of author and publisher, Little, Brown & Co.

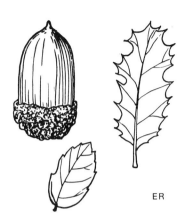

ER

SCRUB OAK *(Quercus dumosa)*

It is my understanding that the Mexican name "Chapparo" applies mainly to the scrub oak, and not to the over all flora such as our derivation of the word "Chaparral" does.

Although the Scrub Oak is responsible for the name Chaparral, it is not the most prolific of the dozen or more shrubs that are true members of the belt. In most cases the Scrub Oak is sparsely inter-mingled with the others, such as Chamise, Sages and Manzanitas, etc.

The Scrub Oak is one of the few shrubs in the Elfin Forest that remains shiny green throughout the year. Some appear to die back in the very arid years, but they recoup after the first rains.

Usually during the heat of summer, a waxy substance is exuded to the upper surface of the leaves, to prevent evaporation, and the leaves bend their edges (margins) down so as to form a sort of upside-down spoon. This is believed done, to present less surface of the leaf to the sun. The leaves, besides being shiny green on the top, are a hairy brownish green beneath. The plant forms a dense growth.

The leaves have forms that are varied. Some leaves are oblong, with small spines along the edges (margins) and are one-half to one and one-half inches long, but the bushes, that are located close to a constant water supply, will often send out leaves three inches long.

The twigs and branches of the true Scrub Oak are strong and leathery, and can cause deep and painful scratches to the skin, even though heavy cloth trousers are worn, if a person tries to force his way through a heavy stand of the scrub. Perhaps the leather chaps worn by the cowboys would be the answer, for that is the reason they wear those seatless breeches, even while riding a horse.

It has been my experience, that on the northern and eastern sides of the hills and small mountains, these oaks will reach a height of 10 feet. On the southern and western or warmer sides of these hills they seldom exceed five to six feet.

It has been estimated that a solid stand of Scrub Oak, about ten years old, and covering an acre, with a good season of rain and sunshine could produce 10 tons of acorns in one year. In August of 1960 we camped at a back country, man-made lake. About forty feet from the lake edge, I spotted a Scrub Oak bush, about 16 feet high, with the entire eastern side covered with a bumper crop of acorns. I took a sheet of newspaper, cut out a square foot of it and hung it at random on the bush. When the photo was blown up, I counted 143 acorns in that square. With a little figuring, I estimated that there were more than 10,000 acorns on that one bush. Certainly a good crop for all the creatures needing winter feed!

Reading about and talking to Indians has shown me they did not like the Scrub Oak acorns, and only used them when there were not enough California Live Oak *(Quercus agrifolia)*. However, when there was a bumper crop of the Scrub Oak acorns, the Indians gathered a quantity, placed them in baskets, and hid them in the arid caves in the high hills of the desert, where they were dried and preserved for years.

The root system of the Scrub Oak is worth noting. A thirty foot cut had been bulldozed into the side of a mountain for a roadway, at about an elevation of 2,300 feet. A small Scrub Oak bush was at the top of this cut, almost on the very edge. The shrub was only about 5 feet high, but the cut had followed the main tap root of the Scrub Oak all the way down to thirty feet! The entire root was exposed the full height of the cut, and still went further down out of sight. This made it a little easier to understand the rapid recuperative powers of this bush after a fire.

The Scrub Oak will be found throughout the foothills of the Elfin Forest up to about 3,000 foot elevation, and often where man has more or less encouraged it, and has developed it into a small tree. That of course means watering and proper pruning. They make excellent shade trees. They seem to grow anywhere the acorn will germinate. They can also be transplanted from one place to another. Take up a lot of their original soil with them and keep well-watered and shaded. With care they can become a real friend around a mountain cabin. I know for I have several around my cabin, and they have been there for 15 years.

POISON OAK *(Rhus diversiloba)*

How this 4 to 20 foot high bush or vine acquired the name of Oak, I do not know, for it actually is a member of the Sumac Family. Regardless of the family, it should be given much respect. It may have been named Oak because the leaves have a sort of oak leaf shape.

Poison Oak will be found in the form of a bush, growing alone, or as a vine that puts out aerial roots and clings to the bark of a tree. The plant prefers partly shady, but warm localities, and is found in many habitats throughout California. Its roots and leaves help form a good loamy soil. The plant is not parasitic.

The leaves are arranged in groups of three leaflets. One leaflet at the end of the stem and two more opposite each other about two inches back from the end leaflet. These leaflets vary in size depending on water supply and sunshine. Most are oblong in shape, with small indentures along the margin of the leaflet, and small lobes, like the Oak leaf. In the spring the leaves are a brilliant green, turning to a deep red in the fall and winter. The plant produces greenish flowers, in small clusters, which droop when the waxy white fruit ripens.

The poisonous substance of the Poison Oak is a yellowish, slightly volatile oil, urushiol, one of the phenols. It occurrs in the sap of the plant and is present in the leaves, flowers, fruit, bark, stems and roots of the plant.

About the best preventive, although sometimes it does not work, is to make a wet lather of yellow laundry soap and use it as a protective film over most exposed parts of the body, the face, hands, arms and legs, particularly the wrists, fingers, and ankles, before going into the field. The more complete the film of soap coats the skin the better the chance that the irritating oil will be washed away in the dissolving soap, when one bathes, after touching the plant.

Recently, various ointments have been developed that contain zirconium. These will often relieve the itching, and have been known to dry up the little blisters. With some people, they have almost no effect. In 1959, a Poison Oak or Poison Ivy "pill" was developed to be used orally. Some people claimed complete immunity, while in others, the reaction amounted to a case of Poison Oak or Ivy. A mulch made by boiling leaves of the Manzanita bush or Madrone tree has been used to prevent itching.

I remember many years back, while I was living in the Sierra Madre Mountains, when I was about 13 years of age, I had a chum who was constantly bothered with Poison Oak. He announced one day that an old Indian had told him that if a person would eat a leaf of the bush, it would make him immune to the poison. I did not agree with him, and tried to talk him out of trying it.

A week later I learned that my chum was in the hospital. I went to his mother and asked what was wrong. She told me, that he would not tell her what he had done, nor would he tell the doctor. Then I told her of his plan to eat a leaf of the Poison Oak. She immediately contacted the doctor. The boy was released from the hospital about two weeks later, after much suffering. That was 40 years ago. I talked to him recently, and asked if the experiment had made him immune. He said it had, for he had not been closer than 50 feet to the bush in 40 years to find out!

A few general suggestions might be in order. Pets that travel in and around these bushes can transport the oil in their fur. Keep them away from children and others who contact the poison easily, until the animal can be given a thorough bath. Shoes and clothes can pick up the oil. Have the clothes cleaned or thoroughly washed, and treat shoes with saddle soap. If Poison Oak branches, leaves or roots are placed on the camp fire, remember the smoke can carry the oil and deposit it on those sitting around the fire. Warn children of the red leaves in the fall and winter as they are very colorful and small children have been known to gather them. In the recreation areas in the Elfin Forest, maintenance crews have thoughtfully removed most of these offensive shrubs.

It is hoped that what has been written here will not make a person over cautious, and afraid of the Elfin Forest. I have tramped over these hills for 40 years, and neither my wife nor I have ever contacted the poison. Most persons who are cautious and avoid contact with it will never notice the effects.

CHAMISE *(Adenostoma fasciculatum)*

From the foothills up to 3,000 foot elevation or better, the Chamise is by far the most prolific and predominant shrub of all the Chaparral. In many cases these bushes form an almost solid thicket for square mile after square mile. Very often when the Chaparral ventures down to the sea, the Chamise will be found to have a good patch down to the edge of the cliffs, that overlook the sea.

The shrub usually grows to a height of three to five feet, forming almost impassable barriers. I have read where early botanists have waded into a patch of the Chamise, and have had great difficulty in getting back into the clear. The shrub has no armament like thorns, but its branches are very stiff and leathery.

The Chamise bears many bunches of short fascicled (clustered or bundled) linear, club shaped leaves that remain attached to the branches, and hold their gray-green color throughout the year. It may be hard to believe, but the Chamise is a member of the rose family. It bears a small whitish flower in a cyme (little flat topped bunches). The new blossoms show up from May to July, and attract many bees and insects. The flowers usually remain attached to their stems throughout the summer, and they turn to a rusty red color. Each blossom produces seeds. The little seeds provide considerable food for the small birds and animals of the Elfin Forest.

The Chamise might be considered the mainstay of the watershed, holding the granite, sandy-like soil together. But also, it is a curse to the brush firefighter, and lives up to its nickname, Greasewood. When a fire is in a thicket of this bush, it burns with intense heat, throwing up black smoke. A little light wind fans a flame into a fast moving fire that often outruns the firefighters. This is mainly caused by a waxy substance exuded by the small linear leaves to protect themselves against the evaporation of their water supply.

As the Chamise ages, the reddish bark foliates or sheds, in long stringy grayish-brown pieces. When the root (burl) is brought to the surface by a bulldozer, it is knurled, and covered with the same shreddy bark as the main stem. These roots may be the size of a volley ball, and make excellent fuel for the campfire.

As usual, the Indians found certain medicinal use of the foliage. An infusion (extraction of a liquid by steeping or soaking) was made for syphilis, and the oil was used as a cure for skin infections. Cattle were fed it when they appeared ill, and it seemed to work. The deadwood was used to start a fast cooking campfire.

MANZANITA *(Arctostaphylos species)*

When one tells about the Manzanita, he speaks of it as a small tree, or a bush, in a general manner, for in the book by Philip A. Munz "A California Flora" there are 51 different species listed. So the following information is more or less general in nature, unless otherwise stated.

They are all evergreen woody plants, varying from low prostrate shrubs to small woody trees. Usually all the branches are crooked, with a thin red or red brown bark that is smooth. The bark is shed in long strips and curls (exfoliating). The leaves are simple, oval-like and alternate along small branches and twigs. In very hot weather these leaves turn on their sides, with the edge of the leaf faced towards the sun. Another example of how a plant keeps its water supply from evaporation! The Manzanita flowers range in color from a pearly white to tinges of rose or pink. They are shaped like inverted bells or urns, with the small open end hanging down. Each blossom usually produces one fruit with a thin layer of pulp around a solid stone.

The scientific name is from Greek, arktos which means bear, and the staphyls meaning a bunch of grapes. When first discovered, it was known as "Bear Grapes". I like the more recent, rather melodic Spanish name; "Manzanita", meaning Little Apple.

The Indians from British Columbia to San Diego had a great deal of respect for the Manzanita. One reason was for the fruits that it bore. They also like the fact that it was not "fire-killed" by brush fires but would send out new shoots from its burl root; hence the belief in reincarnation, as mentioned before. (Not all species of Manzanita have basal burls.)

The small red berries that are produced by the shrub were gathered by the Indians and eaten raw; cooked and ground into meal, and made into a porridge. Actually the Indian considered these berries next to the acorn as a food. Another way they used the berries was to crush and scald them with enough hot water to equal the bulk of the berries. After this mixture had settled, the liquid was considered a fine refreshing drink. This was usually done with the Gray Leaf Manzanita berries (Arctostaphylos Mewukka).

The Indians also found that when the leaves and berries were crushed together they produced certain astringent properties for the relief of bronchitis, dropsy and other diseases. A strong tea made from the berries was considered a relieving wash for Poison Oak. After the white man arrived and showed the Indian how to smoke, the Indian crushed the dried leaves and mixed them with tobacco to swell his supply.

There were, and still may be, several Indian tribes, who would celebrate the ripening of the Manzanita berries with feasts and dancing.

The wood, although few of the branches were straight, was often used in the construction of the Indian huts. The Karok (meaning up-stream) Indian tribe would fashion spoons and food scrapers out of the wood, for scraping acorn soup out of their cooking baskets. Pipes were also made from the wood. The pipes were soaked in eel or bear grease to prevent the wood from splitting.

The shrub is very decorative in the home flower garden, and will prosper in most any kind of soil. It also makes interesting house decorations, either in its natural state or after sand-blasting. There is one thing to remember, however, that the Manzanita is protected by law in both state and federal areas. The best places to collect samples are from gift shops, where they have permits for gathering Manzanita, or from an area that is being cleared for a roadway or firebreak, after permission has been obtained.

The white man has found the berries of the Gray Leaf species (Arctostaphylos Mewukka), make an excellent jelly. Again it is suggested that this be obtained from commercial dealers.

If you wish to learn to recognize the different species, a good botanical book on western plants and shrubs should be consulted.

YUCCA, *species*

If November, December and January produce the amount of rain needed, and the sun cooperates with the proper quantity and quality of rays to stir to life that spark of propagation in the seed, from late January through May, the crowning, jewel-like beauty of the Chaparral will spring out in all its glory, the Whipple Yucca.

Much has been written about this plant that lifts its sturdy green shaft above the monotonous tops of its Chaparral companions. Then as though by command, the pinnacle of the stalk bursts into pearly white blooms, having a delicate floral perfume.

The glory of this member of the Agave family (meaning "noble") in Greek), is illustrated by the common local names given it. "The Lord's Candle", "Our Lord's Candle", etc. Some refer to the Yucca as the "Quixote Plant", for what reason I do not know, unless it is associated with the famous fictional character's spear.

The Yucca is known to most all Californians and especially to travelers who have passed through the Chaparral area during the blossoming period. The plant grows at 1,000 to 4,000 foot elevation from the Santa Lucia, San Jacinto and Santa Ana Mountains down into Lower California.

Even after the Yucca has completed its cycle of life; blooming, bearing fruit, and maturing seed, lifeless flower stalks continue to stand, blackened by the elements, as though resentful of relinquishing the over-seeing position held through an eventful life.

In the years when the Model "T" Ford touring automobile was the predominant family car, the proud Yucca stalks were lashed to the sides of cars, after the traditional Sunday drive. The Yucca usually was shown to friends, but was in the trash by Tuesday. Certainly this was a sad fate for so majestic a masterpiece of Mother Nature's. Now, however, all the Yuccas are protected by naturalists.

The plant's 8 to 15 foot tall, stalk-like, narrow stem rises from a well-protected base of two or three foot-long fleshy, narrow, spine-tipped leaves; the central shaft ending in a large spike of creamy-white blossoms.

The Indians found many uses for the species. A strong thread-like cord was made from the long spear-like leaves. The Yucca leaves were usually soaked in water; then laid on a rock and beaten with a wooden beater; washed often in water to remove the pulp; and beaten again, until the lateral fibers were all that were left. These fibers were strong and pliable. They were used to sew together rabbit and deer skins to make blankets and clothing. Some of the fibers were used as bow strings, and often their huts were tied together with these cords. In the 1800's these Yucca fibers were woven into ropes, made into fishing nets, hats, hairbrushes, and horse blankets.

The stalks contain a quantity of sugar. The Indians of Arizona, New Mexico, and Mexico fermented these stalks and made them into an alcoholic drink.

The color of the Yucca fiber was dependent upon the kind of species it was and where it was grown. These fibers were used mostly in the decoration of ceremonial costumes. Paint brushes for painting the face and clothing were also made from these Yucca fibers.

The many species of the Yucca provided a variety of food. Indians, deer, birds and insects all vied for the fruit. The Indians would often gather the fruit (seed capsules) while still green to prevent them being taken by the others, and ripen them in the sun. The green fruit was cooked and eaten. The ripe fruit could be eaten raw, but more often it was boiled or roasted over hot coals. Sometimes the fruit was skinned, and the seeds removed; then the fruit was worked into a paste and spread on mats made of grass and allowed to dry, sometimes for several weeks. This was then reworked and finally formed into blocks or cakes, and dried. These blocks were stored in a dry place for winter use. (And we think we discovered dehydrated food!) The blocks had a further use, as an item for barter with other tribes.

The roots, of some species, were used to make a primitive soap and a shampoo. Also part of the large stem or the root was carefully burned and the ash was used to make a blue-black dye. This dye was used to tattoo one's person with the aid of a sharp thorn from a cactus.

With all of these fascinating things that have been written about the Yucca, there just does not seem to be much more to add, but there is still the most fascinating story of all, how the Yucca is fertilized.

There is a unique relationship between the plant and the Pronuba (*Tegeticula*) or Yucca Moth. This white, ¼" to a little over an inch in length moth   is not a mere nectar sipper, like so many other insects that visit the flower, but rather the link between the survival of the species of the plant or its possible extinction.   It is the only known means by which the flower of the Yucca is fertilized.

The female Pronuba Moth enters the Yucca flower when it is ready to be fertilized, gathers pollen, in its modified mouth, then using its ovipositor (an organ at the end of the abdomen by which eggs are deposited) stabs the ovary of the flower, inserting its egg directly into the ovary.

This is more or less a common process to several insects, but the next act of the wee moth, although I suppose it is instinctive, seems to display an almost uncanny knowledge of botany.   After the egg has been deposited, the moth then takes the pollen to the top of the pistol and pushes it down into the funnel shaped stigma.   The pistol is the organ that contains the ovary at its base and the ovary contains the egg.   The stigma is the top of the pistol.   The little female moth takes neither nectar nor pollen for herself, but performs the one act that will guarantee the proper food for the larva which will develop from the egg.

The Yucca will of course, lose a few seeds, but what a small price for such a necessary service.   After the larva has developed, it will leave the seed and pod and develop as a cocoon, finally becoming a moth about the time the Yuccas are ready to bloom the following season.   Certainly this is a most remarkable association between plant and insect life!

This association was first discovered by a Professor Riley in 1872. Professor Riley's papers may be found in the publications of the St. Louis Academy of Science, and in the 4th and 5th volumes of his books, "Insect Life".

If you wish to see the Pronuba Moth at work, you will have to watch it at night.   During the daylight hours the moth spends its time hidden in the Yucca flower.   At nightfall it becomes active, since it is a nocturnal being.   Most insects have ceased their activities and this of course, eliminates a great deal of interruption while the pronuba is performing such a delicate operation for its existence. Most of the species do rely on the same insects for fertilization.   For example, the *Pronuba maculata* pollenates the *Yucca Whipplei*.

Yes, the more you investigate the Elfin Forest the more fascinating it becomes.

DODDER VINE

In the early spring, one of the first colors that makes a show in the rather drab coloring of the Chaparral is the treacherous Dodder Vine. These appear as blotches of beautiful brilliant orange.

Dodder Vine, alias Devil's Thread, has the generic name of *Cuscuta*. At least 21 different species are found in the Elfin Forest, the upper forest zones, and the cultivated fields. All are parasitic and contain no chlorophyll [the green colored matter used for the process of photosynthesis to convert water and carbon dioxide into glucose (plant starch) which is then broken down into the by-products for food for the plant cells].

The fascinating thing about the Dodder Vine is that it is a true flowering plant, and each year in the early spring, following the rains, the seeds that were produced the past year come to life as new plants. As soon as this germination takes place and the shoot of the new plant comes to the surface of the soil, it seeks a normal plant, as it must have food to live above ground.

When this colorful tangled vine reaches its selected host plant or shrub, it starts to climb up the trunk, attaching itself with knob-like haustoria (the Latin word meaning "to drink"), sucker-like organs, and starts to feed and grow. When this connection has been well established, that part of the vine that came from the soil dries up and fades away in a day or two. Then the Dodder is wholly dependent upon the host plant.

If the summer is very dry, and the Dodder Vines mature, the host plant is unable to support them both; so the host dies. But in many cases where a neighboring plant or shrub has in some way intertwined itself with the dying plant, the Dodder Vine will quickly attach itself to that plant and continue to enjoy the new source of food and water. A Dodder Vine attaches to as many as four different host plants at one time.

The various species of the Dodder family, have many host plants that they will attach to, native shrubs and small trees included. One type of Dodder will confine its "free-loading" tactics to marsh plants.   Another species accidently introduced from Chile, causes considerable damage to the cultivated Alfalfa.

It is interesting that the very matter that the Dodder Vine does not have, chlorophyll, can be found only in green plants, shrubs and trees, and all life depends upon this matter, including man! Cattle obtain the benefits of chlorophyll when they eat grass and hay. Mammals depend upon it directly or indirectly.

The Dodder Vine has very small waxy white flowers during May through October which produce two small seeds that fall to the ground and germinate the following year. Very tiny scale-like leaves can be seen with a magnifying glass.

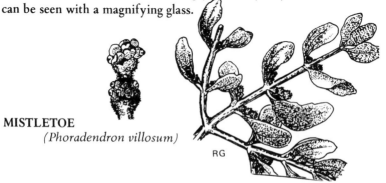

MISTLETOE
(Phoradendron villosum)

RG

Another parasitic plant in the Elfin Forest is the Mistletoe. Some botanists consider it as only a partial parasite, because it does contain chlorophyll, and when it attaches itself to a woody plant or tree as a host, it is mainly seeking water, as it does not have any connection with the ground, and no means of retaining rain water. As with the Dodder, if the Mistletoe's demands become too much, the host will eventually die.

The Mistletoe bears a seed coated in a sticky substance. Birds like this seed coating. The birds cannot digest the seed and thus it is planted in the trees by their droppings. If the seed is not eaten it may fasten itself to a bird's feathers and then be rubbed off by the bird on to another limb of a tree where it will adhere and eventually germinate. The Mistletoe's growth is easily identified by a clump of green up in a tree or large bush, mostly those which are near a source of water, either above or below the soil.

About the only good I can think of in the Mistletoe, is its appearance in the home on the top of the door casing along about Christmas time and in a house full of pretty girls!

INDIAN PAINT BRUSH *(Castilleja species)*

There is still another parasitic plant, that, from all outside appearances, gives no indication of its underground activities. This is the Indian Paintbrush and its several closely related cousins. The approach is very different in this case. They make their connection with the host's roots. This again may be called a partial parasite, for all it is after is water. In some cases it has been beneficial to its host. If the host plant has been closely cropped by deer or cattle, the Paint Brush seems to help the host plant to survive by conserving the surplus water. This enables the host plant to get a fresh start with new sprouted leaves.

GALLS

Galls are sometimes referred to as parasitic. However, they should be considered as an abnormal growth on the plant. Many of the Galls are caused by insects. Other Galls are caused by bacteria, virus, nematodes, fungi, injury, etc. A Gall forms, but exactly why no one really knows for sure. If caused by an insect the Gall provides food and housing for the egg and the development of the small maggot in the spring. When the maggot has matured, it eats its way out of the gall-apple. These galls are found on Oak, Goldenrod and Blackberry bushes to name a few.

CHAPTER 6

TREES OF THE CHAPARRAL

CALIFORNIA LIVE OAK

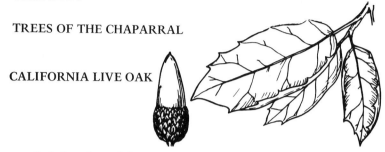

I feel that the California Live Oak *(Quercus agrifolia*—pronounced "kwer-cus-aggruh-foal-ee-uh"), although classed as a tree, should be mentioned with the other members of the Elfin Forest. Variation *frutescens Engelmann* is a shrub form occurring in Chaparral.

Most botanists do not include full grown trees as part of the Chaparral, but it cannot be very well denied when the Chaparral grows all around a tree.

The early British explorer Vancouver once wrote of the Oak along the western coast, "Stately Lords of the Forest". We do not know of what Oak species he was writing, for there are many kinds in the area, however, at least to me, in an imaginative way, the California Live Oak is the King of the Elfin Forest.

The botanical history of the California Live Oak indicates that it was possibly the first tree specimen of California to be taken to Europe in about 1791 by the members of the Malaspina Expedition. The specimen was turned over to Née ; an 18th-19th century botanist who had not come to this Coast, but he was the first to describe and name the tree. The early Spanish already had given the tree a common name, "Encina" and associated it with the properties of fertility. They considered the trees desirable around a location for a residence. The Franciscan founders of the Missions closely followed this theory in the narrow Chaparral belt and coastal areas of California from San Francisco south.

In the area south of Los Angeles, California Live Oak will be found on valley floors and up to an elevation of 3,000 feet. Occasionally a lone tree will be spotted on a hillside. In many recreational spots, such as camp grounds and picnic facilities, this oak provides much of the shade. In many of these areas they form a grove of 25 to 75 trees. Since the tree is usually wider than it is high, it provides considerable shade. The usual height for a mature tree is 35 to 65 feet while it will often be as much as 75 or more feet broad. The trunk rises singly from 6 to 12 feet high, and then branches out with large limbs. The limbs are often twisted and gnarled, making the tree almost useless as a lumber source. It is not unusual to find several trunks rising from one root system. The trunk grows up to, but rarely exceeds 4 feet in diameter. The trunk bark of the older trees is often furrowed and forms irregular plates. The young trees and limbs have a bark that is smooth and lead gray. Sometimes on the younger trees, the bark looks as though it had been pulled on like a stocking, showing the folds in the wood beneath.

The California Live Oak is readily identified by several distinctive features. The leaves are evergreen, dropping the older leaves and replacing them with new ones the year around. The leaves are oval to oblong. The top of the leaf is polished green with an underside of yellowish-green. The mid-rib and veins are clearly visible. The young leaves are often flat, but after a few months they take the shape of an inverted teaspoon, curving down at the margins towards the undersides of the leaves. As the leaf gets older, it will start to form small brown spines at each lobe or scallop of the margin. This caused early explorers to nickname the tree "Holly Oak".

It may be hard to imagine an Oak Tree in full bloom, but it does happen. During April through June, the "Southland Spring", there is a sudden burst of new growth of leaves, reddish-purple and green, and coming out of the ends of all the branches and twigs. From this new growth, downy spikes of tiny flowers or florets, (catkins) appear, The male catkin is limp, drooping and willowy, yellowish green in color, from 1 to 2½ inches in length. The female flower is more rigid, greenish with only a hint of yellow. A five (5-X) power magnifying glass shows the individual flowers. Male florets have 2 to 6 stamens composed of filaments with anthers. The stamens are the male part of the flower. The anthers produce the fertilizing pollen. The pistillate or female flowers form a solitary tube, in a many bracted involucre (a cupule, similar to an unopened rosebud). The involucre eventually forms the cup of the acorn.

As a final identification of the tree, the acorn is distinctive. Including the cup and nut, the acorn will vary from ½ inch to nearly 2 inches long, depending upon the amount of rainfall received. The scaly brown cup covers about one quarter of the nut. The acorn is slim, coming to a sharp brown point. The base of the acorn is dark to light green. It is all brown when mature. WARNING—do not eat these nuts as they contain considerable tannin. This can cause violent vomiting. The Indians did not eat these nuts until they had been thoroughly leached. The acorns appear in late summer and early fall. If not gathered by squirrels, woodpeckers, or broken open by the Blue Jays they fall to the ground in October through December.

A similar Oak, *Quercus agrifolia (variety) oxyadenia* can be distinguished with a magnifying glass. The underside of the leaves have stellate (star-shaped) clusters of fine hairs.

Here are a few interesting facts about the Oak Trees, collected at random—many Oaks live for 1,500 years, and have as much as 100 miles of roots in their system. There are about 200 species of Oaks, more than any other tree species. About 60 species are in cultivation. A full grown Oak Tree has an estimated 700,000 leaves! An average Indian family required 500 pounds of acorns in a year when they were a major part of their diet. Southern California Indians preferred the California Live Oak acorns to any other, for their taste, when leached. Northern California Indians prefer the tan bark acorn *(Lithocarpus densiflora)*. Acorns were often gathered in the Chaparral, and taken to the high desert mountain caves, and stored in baskets there. The dry desert air preserved them for centuries. Some have been discovered recently in perfect condition, believed over 200 years old.

SYCAMORE *(Platanus racemosa)*

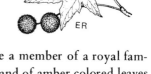

It stands majestic, tall and slender, like a member of a royal family! Each year, in the fall it sheds the garland of amber colored leaves from its loose crown of branches, and slips graciously out of its last summer's wrap of brown bark.

In the spring as entitles a Chaparral queen, the bloom of tiny flowers returns to the loose crownand the new leaves form a glorious green hair-do, marcelled by the dainty fingers of the spring breeze. Truly fit for a queen! The trunk has a skin-tight garb of a pale-gray to a pale green sometimes showing yellow and brown blotches.

Albert Kellogg (1813-1887), a San Francisco physician and botanist, wrote about the tree as the "wonderful majesty".

For me in thinking of the Elfin Forest, I certainly nominate the Sycamore as its queen, Her Majesty.

The correct pronunciation of the Latin name, *Platanus racemosa,* is (Pla-ta-nus-rass-uh-mo-suh). A number of common names apply such as Western or California Sycamore, Button Tree, Buttonball Tree, Plane Tree, and Aliso Tree. Another similar species is the popular street-side "London Plane Tree", *(Platanus acerifolia).*

The Sycamore tree in the Chaparral belt is usually found along the banks of running or intermittent running streams. Someone once called it "the ghost that stands with its feet in water". The tree is found throughout various parts of California and is hardy in Southern California. It usually will be found in company with other trees like the Alders, Willows, Box Elders and Oaks.

Most generally, the foliage is light, and in the winter the tree becomes bare. Often a few seed "buttons" may remain hanging to a branch of the tree. Crack one of these buttons open, and you will be surprised to find the seeds have a fuzz on them, much like the dandelion. In the spring these balls will break open and spread their seeds with the help of the winds.

The leaves are five pointed, looking like the Maple leaf, lobed rather deeply, thick and leathery, a pale green-yellow above and a paler color beneath. They are not polished like so many other Chaparral leaves. The leaf has brownish underleaf hairs that slough off. Often I have watched the Humming Birds gather this moss-like substance, using it to line their nests. The Indians also found a use for these hairs. They would carefully scrape the hairs off the leaves, and mix them with the boiled dry yolk of a quail's egg and use it to relieve catarrh. The leaves are from five to ten inches long and equally as wide and are borne five to six on each twig.

The seed clusters in spiked "buttonballs", grow to one inch in diameter. The spikes are firm but not rigid to the extent that they are untouchable. There are two to seven of these greenish balls hanging from a stem, six to ten inches long. As stated before, the blossoms are very small and are well protected by the base of the leaf, instead of the normal covering of scales (sepals).

The tree's main trunk seldom grows straight up. On close inspection of the bark, in springtime, it will be noted to almost spiral upward. This makes the splitting of the wood for fuel most difficult. Some enthusiastic carpenter will turn the Sycamore on his lathe, showing to advantage the delightful grain of the wood with its brown streaks. This wood finishes up so beautifully. The tree seldom grows a single trunk, but usually two to three trunks will grow from one root system. The main trunk grows to and rarely exceeds 2 to 3 feet in diameter at the base.

Incidentally, this Sycamore is not the species noted in the Bible *(Fiscus sycomorus)*, as some botanists have not made clear. However, it is of the same general family, *(Platanaceae)*.

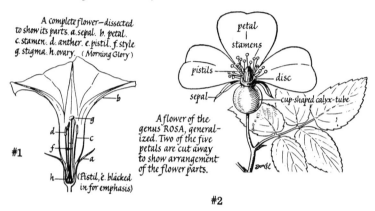

#1 and #2.   Two typical flowers, showing the names of their parts.

Taken from The Amateur Naturalist Handbook by Vinson Brown, artist Donald Kelley, by permission of author and publisher, Little, Brown & Co.

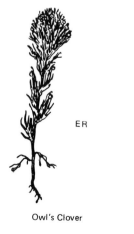

Owl's Clover

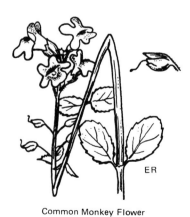

Common Monkey Flower

CHAPTER 7

DISCOVERY OF WILD FLOWER GEMS

*

ER

After consideration of how to present the Wild Flowers of the Elfin Forest I realized that it was an impossibility to do the subject true justice for several reasons. One reason is the list of plants is very long. In San Diego County alone, the botanists at the Museum of Natural History have compiled a list of more than 1,400 species and varieties. My list of Wild Flowers over the past ten years, is just a bit short of 400.

The second reason would involve the timing of your visit. It is almost an impossibility to list those flowers that you will come in contact with first and most often. If you enter the Elfin Forest at one point during the early spring you may come in contact with Owl's Clover, *(Orthocarpus purpurescens)*, then a few months later you will find a profusion of Yellow Monkey Flowers *(Mimulus species)*. Come to the forest at another place and you will observe still another flower. The communities of wild flowers vary for so many reasons, soil, water availability, shade or sun exposure, and time of the year.

Thirdly, it is beyond the scope of this book to provide such lengthy lists, when there are many fine knowledgeable books available. See reference list at the end of the book.

True identification of Wild Flowers can be accomplished with patience and a knowledge of the typical flower parts and types of flower formations. Leaf forms and arrangements should be learned. See sketches on pages 24, 42, and 45.

For an additional help with colors, I obtained a chart from a child's coloring book. It has served well in my work with flowers as with bird identification. Most paint store charts contain patent specialized colors that do not match natural colors, and are only relevant to their products.

The personal note book is important. If you feel you want to wax a bit poetic or over-descriptive, do it, since you don't have to show the notebook to anyone else. More than 70% of this book is taken

* Owl's Clover

from notes made in the field, over the past 10 years, and also includes notes taken when I was a more observant 14 year old.

A small loose leaf notebook is most helpful. I always carry this book in my pocket. I would make brief notes, then when I arrived home, I would smooth out these notes in a regular school composition loose leaf folder. These notes became a part of an accumulation of very crude pencil sketches, photographs, charts and notes of authoritative writers. The public library is one of my best sources of additional information.

While looking for Wild Flowers I usually carry very simple gear, such as:

1. A note book with a reminder form of what to look for. (see the sample form at the end of this chapter).

2. Several pencils.

3. A single edged razor blade, or thin bladed, very sharp pen knife.

4. A good 5 to 10 times magnifying glass.

5. A good guide book.

6. One or two pairs of tweezers.

With these few tools of the trade, I have spent many pleasant week-ends in the Elfin Forest. It could have been one of just frustration; chasing lost kids, reading a stale day old Sunday paper; or calling a city bred dog back to camp and convincing him that skunks and squirrels were not cats to be chased, and rattlesnakes and boas were not toys.

The family suddenly became an interested group, and wanted to know what I was finding out. It led to long bird watching trips and hikes. It was not too long until I found that the children who went on these camping trips with us knew more birds and wild flowers by just seeing them along the trails, than I did. The children's parents told us, that their children were getting better marks on their compositions in school. It's remarkable how youngsters can become so efficient in observation, and remember what they have seen.

One final word. Flower and plant pressing in past years was an interesting hobby. It also turned out to be a disappointing one. Usually the flower colors faded. If mounted in a loose leaf folder, the turning of the pages broke the plant's stems and leaves. In time certain insects made their attack, and then the whole thing became a mess and the housekeeper rightfully ordered the remains to the trash barrel. If you are blessed with the ability to make simple line draw-ings or can take photos in color or black and white, you are in luck and will have a permanent record.

In the past 10 years I have followed the FLOWER OBSERVA-TION CHART that I devised. True, I have not been able to fill in all the blanks while in the field, but what notes I did gather have helped in the final study when at home again with my books and other forms of identification material.

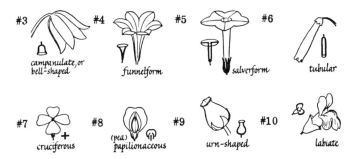

#3 to #10. Types of Flowers. #3 and #4 are apetalous, which means without distinct petals and sepals; #7 and #8 are choripet-alous, which means the petals and sepals are each completely free from each other; #5, 6, 9 and 10 are sympetalous, which means the petals and sepals are all more or less closely joined together.

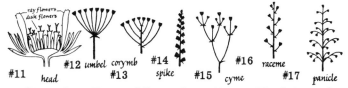

#11 to #17. Types of flower formations. The daisy and sun-flower look like single flowers, but really are heads of flowers (#11).

Taken from The Amateur Naturalist Handbook by Vinson Brown, artist Donald Kelley, by permission of author and publisher, Little, Brown & Co.

FLOWER OBSERVATION FORM

1. Common Name_____

2. Scientific Name_____ 3. Species_____

4. Genus_____ 5. Family_____

6. Date_____7. Locality_____8. Time____

9. Type Season (dry-wet) 10. Weather_____

11. Flower (Type) (a) Monocots_____(b) Decots_____

12. Calyx (a) Color_____(b) Arrangement_____

13. Sepals (Number) (a) Size in inches (b)Length____(c) Width____

14. Corolla (a) Color_____(b)Arrangement _____

    (c) Size - Length_____Width_____(c) No. of Petals_____

    (e) Shape_____(d) Texture_____

15. Stamens (a) Color_____ (b) Length_____ (c) Number____

    (d) Filament Color_____ (e) Anther Color_____

16. Pistil (a) Color_____ (b) Length_____(c) Number_____

    (d) Style Color_____ (e) Stigma Color _____

17. Flowershape_____(a) Flower size_____

18. Leaf (a) Color_____(b) Size (Length) (Width)_____

    (c) Thickness_____(d) Shape _____

    (e) Type_____(f) Leaf edge_____

    (g) Leaf arrangement_____(h) Leaf appearance (bottom)_____

    (i) Top _____(j) Other_____

19. Roots (a) Fibrous_____(b) Tap_____(c) Tuberous_____

FLOWER OBSERVATION CHART (cont.)

20. Stem or Stalk: (a) Prickly _____(b) Smooth_____

    (c) Soft_____(d) Brittle_____(e) Color _____

    (f) Thickness _____(g) Other_____

21.Fruit: Color_____ Size – Length_____Width_____

    Shape_____Nut-like_____Pod _____

    Capsule_____Other_____

22. Seeds: Color_____Size Diam____Width_____ Length_____

    Shape: Pea_____ Oblong _____Winged _____

    Fuzzy_____ Other_____

General Notes: _____

Height of Plant (Mature)_____

Where Found: Roadside _____Bog____ Dense Forest_____

            Open Thicket_____ Pasture_____Field_____

            Beach _____Creek or River Bank_____

            Creek or River Bed_____Hillside _____

            Facing (approx.) N_____S_____E_____W_____

Soil: Type_____Sandy_____Humus_____

    Condition: Dry_____Damp_____

    Growing with (Other Plants) Name_____

    Insects or birds that visit plant_____

    Further notes (Pictures taken) at _____

      Sketches_____

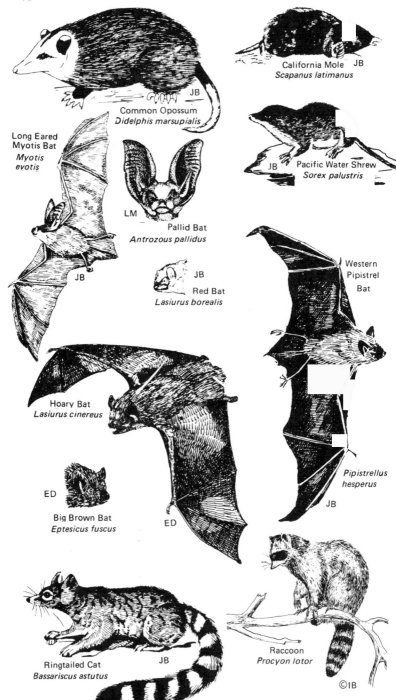

Common Opossum
Didelphis marsupialis
JB

California Mole   JB
Scapanus latimanus

Long Eared
Myotis Bat
*Myotis
evotis*

Pacific Water Shrew
Sorex palustris
JB

Pallid Bat
Antrozous pallidus
LM

JB

Red Bat
Lasiurus borealis
JB

Western
Pipistrel
Bat

Hoary Bat
Lasiurus cinereus

*Pipistrellus
hesperus*
JB

Big Brown Bat
Eptesicus fuscus
ED

ED

Ringtailed Cat
Bassariscus astutus
JB

Raccoon
Procyon lotor

©IB

CHAPTER 8

MAMMALS IN THE ELFIN FOREST

The number and variety of mammals in the Elfin Forest is amazing. Actually the Chaparral is alive with life of many sorts, but the casual observer sees scarcely any. The first reason for this is that many of the animals are nocturnal in their habits, and secondly most are very timid and remain in their hiding places even when they have a suspicion that a human being or enemy is near by. And finally, most of these creatures are smaller than an adult tom cat, and their fur colors blend into nothingness against the background of their habitat.

But then on the other hand, there are a number of these "beasties" who seem bent on making show-offs of themselves. You simply can't help but see them! For example, most all the Squirrels in the Elfin Forest are real hams.

BEECHEY GROUND SQUIRREL
(Otospermophilus beecheyi)

JB

One thing I am sure of is that the California or Beechey Ground Squirrel has never been convinced that he couldn't beat any automobile made in a race. In the spring it is a common sight to see one of these little fellows sitting on his haunches, body bolt upright, watching as you approach the dirt drain ditch at the side of the road. When in HIS opinion your car is even with him, he drops to all fours and furiously scampers down the ditch for fifty to a hundred feet. When he feels that he has won the race, he skips out of the ditch into the brush where his home is.

This squirrel is easily identified. The body is 9-11 inches long and has a 5-9 inch long tail. The body is reddish-brown with a few flecks of buffy-white on the back. The underside is buff. The Beechey ground squirrel hibernates during the winter.

* Pinyon Mouse, *Peromyscus truei* .

When seen around boulders and rock piles he is often called the
Rock Squirrel, but this is the name of a similar squirrel found in the
mountains of the Mohave Desert. He is noticed from early spring
until late fall. By the time that you do see these little actors, they
will have already been watching you, for they usually are located on
the very top of the boulder or pile of rocks, sitting on their haunches.
They have been alerted, and from their vantage place, are keeping
watch. The best time to see these quaint, watchful fellows is after 10
in the morning and before 4 in the afternoon. These sentries of the
Elfin Forest are usually all gray, but with dark markings. The tail is
the finest adornment, often held high. For a moment, the little animal appears motionless, but if you approach too close, the end of the
tail starts to twitch. As you get closer the tail works from side to
side, and suddenly shoots straight up, and then he is off like a streak,
usually headed for his hole under the boulders.

I have read several accounts by naturalists in which they have said
that the one squirrel is on watch for possible intruders, for a group
of animals, while other naturalists state frankly that the squirrels
are simple show-offs. Other authorities claim that these squirrels
are acting as decoys to steer the intruder away from their nests. In
the latter case one squirrel usually appears on the top of a boulder or
rock pile away from his own home. As far as I have been able to as-
certain the question (whether they are protectors or show-offs) is
still unanswered and perhaps YOU can find out. There are many
worthwhile questions to be answered about nature.

If I can't see one of the Beechey Squirrels watching me, all I have
to do is toss a small stone at a rock pile where I have seen a squirrel
before, and in a matter of moments one of the regulars will appear.
Too, if you are looking at a squirrel through a pair of field glasses,
remember to remain motionless and so will he. In the winter these
little fellows cease to perform, give up their sentry duty, and hiber-
nate or estivate underground.

SPOTTED SKUNK *(Spilogale putorius)*

VC

The Little Stinker is both a familiar resident of the forest, and menace to chickens and motorists. When the Spotted Skunk visits an im-
properly fenced chicken yard, mere words cannot tell the damage he
can do, besides, leaving his scented calling card. Dead chickens, brok-
en eggs and thoroughly disheveled setting hens also abound.

The real menace is found when driving in the back country, on
little traveled roads. An example is the story of my friend who purchased a small place of about five Chaparral acres in the foothills.
He was half-way up the half-mile long driveway to his new place, in
his brand new station wagon. One of the family spied a small Spotted Skunk, gazing down at them. The headlights were blinding the
little fellow. From the back seat came the childish cry—

"Run over him, Daddy, he'll kill our chickens".

Daddy swerved ever so slightly. They felt the bump. It was too
late! He had reacted on reflex action without thinking.

Soon it was evident that Daddy had been hasty. The deed had been
done. The odor of the little spotted beast became stronger. Everyone
was glad to get out of the station wagon when they pulled up in front
of the closed and shuttered farm house. The family went inside and
threw open all of the windows and shutters to let in the fresh air.
Soon it seemed that the car was parked in the wrong place, for the
odor was everywhere. Daddy went out and unloaded the car, and
drove it into a nearby unplowed field, where the wind and breeze took
the odor away from the house. It sat there for three weeks, before
the family could douse the inside and underside of the car with
enough deodorant to make it bearable to ride in the car. People who
get in the car today, two years later always seem to remark after a
few sniffs, "Skunk".

So in all due respect to Mr. Spotted Skunk, and to your better
judgement, it is better to aim to miss him!

This little fellow has more or less been insulted by the people of
the Deep South for they have nick-named it the "Phoby Cat". This
was short for "Hydrophobia Cat" and implied it was a constant carrier of the dreaded disease. This is not true. It is no more a carrier
than any other animal. This theory perhaps developed because of

the animals' actions during their mating season, when they seem to border on insanity with their antics. In this condition they have been known to attack coyotes and wolves in their dens, chasing out the adults and injuring the cubs. However, any change in normal behavior or strange and unusual behavior of a wild animal should put a person on his guard to use extra caution. The disease, caused by a virus, is prevalent temporarily throughout the western hemisphere at times in bats, dogs, foxes and skunks. All warm blooded animals are susceptible to it.

The Spotted Skunk's body is 9-14 inches long, with an additional 4½ to 9 inches to the bushy tail. They weigh only 1 to 2 pounds. The hair accentuates their size. They are carnivorous (flesh eating); their diet includes insects, worms, mice and some plants. They perhaps kill many more pests in the field, than chickens in the yard, but the chicken is such an easy prey, on the roost; and hen eggs are so tempting!

I shall give the markings, but hope that you won't try to get close enough to see them. It has a white spot on the forehead, one under each ear, and four broken white stripes along its neck and back. The markings often give the impression of being striped, like their bigger cousins, which have unbroken lines. The tail has a white tip. These marks may vary considerably. I made my close up observations in a zoo. It was much safer.

Apparently these little fellows are reluctant to use their foul smelling scent spray, for they usually give a warning. First the skunk turns toward you and stomps the ground with its front paws. If this is not enough, the spotted skunk will do a perfect stand, balancing on his front paws; then with the white tipped tail held high, it will let fly two fine sprays of yellow fluid, that both man and beast abhor.

After all, these little beasts cannot be blamed for what they do, since they are not quick of motion, or as cunning as other creatures. The scent spray is their only defense against animals who find it necessary to challenge them. However, the spotted skunk is much quicker and more agile and frolicsome than its bigger cousin. Like most of the Elfin Forest children, they finally tire of the nocturnal antics, and in winter will hunt for an abandoned burrow, and curl up in a deep sleep when the weather gets too cold.

BRUSH RABBIT *(Sylvilagus bachmani)*

LM

Like many places in the world, the Elfin Forest has its share of rabbits and hares. In this forest, the Brush Rabbit is more predominant. This little fellow is about the size of an adult cat, 11 to 13 inches along, and is usually a shade of brown that blends almost perfectly with the bushy habitat of his home. The ears and tail, compared to other rabbits, are relatively small.

The Brush Rabbit prefers the dense brush normally, but in the early morning and evening will cautiously venture out a conservatively safe distance where a quick scurry will take him back to the security of his bush. It seems odd, but contrary to the children's story, not all rabbits have the agility to hop. More often, if observed closely, they inch forward on their front paws, and then bring the two rear paws up together, giving the impression of a hop.

I had always thought that Brush Rabbits were an easy meal for most forest beasts of prey. This I now doubt, after a tussle I saw between one of these little fellows and a young gopher snake. I was descending a small barren hillock, when I saw a female Brush Rabbit tending her litter. I took out my binoculars and focused on the little family. No sooner had I settled down when I spotted a small gopher snake, sneaking through the dry grass, from my direction, and into the wind. That was his first error. My instinct was to try and chase off the snake and save the little family. But at the very moment I was about to dash forward, the Brush Rabbit rose on her haunches, a position I had never seen them take. She looked directly at the slithering reptile. Then suddenly she sprang into the air and landed squarely on the back of the neck of the snake. With her front paws on the young snake, she let loose a barrage of cutting slashes with her hind legs. The snake immediately used all the evasive action of its agile body to remove himself from those cutting feet. He left a bloody trail as he disappeared into a clump of dry leaves. Mrs. Rabbit rushed back to the exposed nest, to see that everything was all right.

The incident reminded me of a few of the bouts I had gone through with some of the bucks in our rabbit menagerie and the nasty cuts they had inflicted on my forearm with their hind feet. I could well understand how the young gopher snake must have felt. "And Mama had said it was so easy to find a nice rabbit dinner", he must have thought. This was the only time I have ever seen a rabbit fight so furiously, and I may never see it again, nor have I ever convinced any one that I saw it happen. But it is a good example of what can happen when one is sharp of eye, alert, and has a good pair of field glasses, and of course has his note book close at hand.

Often, however, these timid bundles of fur are not so fortunate. The Red-tailed and Cooper Hawks that attack from the sky are the most formidable foes. Silently they swoop down and attack with no warning. The one thing the hawk has not been able to overcome is its own shadow. Watch a flock of chickens or a covey of quail when a hawk's shadow passes, and see how they seek shelter. It is not unusual here in Southern California for a low cloud or high fog to cover much of the area. Then the adult hawks take to the air, and carry out their hunting without hindrance. The Barn Owls, Bobcats, Coyotes, Gray Foxes, Weasels, Housecats and etc. are other predatory enemies of the rabbit. Add, of course, the man with his gun and the boy with his sling shot and B-B guns.

The Brush Rabbits are prolific parents. Even though their life is seldom more than three to six years, there seem to be plenty of them. A female will produce three or four litters a year.

BLACKTAILED JACK RABBIT
(Lepus californicus)

The Blacktailed Jack Rabbit or Hare might well be considered a direct opposite of the little Brush Rabbit. The little fellow prefers the seclusion of the heavy bush, while the Jack is a resident of the open field. He is a much larger animal, measuring from head to tail 17 to 21 inches, and sporting ears as long as 6 to 7 inches. The weight of the Jack depends greatly on the availability of food. Under normal conditions they will weigh 3 to 7 pounds.

This hare's antics are comical. Watch one for a time. If it is startled by a snapping twig, it will shoot almost straight up into the air in a mighty jump. It has always been my theory that this is done so it can have a look to determine the cause of the noise. The Jack Rabbit's next move, after he lands, depends upon his view. If pursuit is imminent, off he goes in great bounds that have been measured from 12 to 15 feet. This is the main defence of the Jack Rabbit, his leaping coupled with speed. With little effort, he can outrun the swift coyote or fox. Being of a stubborn nature, he does not always head for shelter or an abandoned burrow. Instead he usually remains on a straight course.

Often when a chase is first started, the fox or coyote takes off at a furious pace, that lasts for a hundred yards or more. Then the larger animal might stop and watch the rabbit, and when it thinks the rabbit is far enough away the predator might slowly slink off to the right or left, about 25 yards or more, find a comfortable spot under a bush, and lay down with an eye on the fleeing rabbit. That is the first phase of a chase; the next phase is left up to the rabbit, and he may accommodate the predator.

The Jack will usually continue to bound along until he is tired and winded. When he stops, he will usually look and listen in the direction of his pursuer, and satisfy himself the chase is over. Often after a short rest he hops off in a large U turn, and HEADS right back from whence he came. Also, this was exactly the strategy that had been planned by the predator, and will net the awaiting animal a fine repast. Brains and cunningness many times win over speed.

Breeding continues the year around with the Jack Rabbits. This prolificness provides much food for the Coyotes, Housecats, Bob Cats, Horned Owls, various Hawks and etc. Some people say that the killing of these innocent little creatures is cruel. However, where the predator of a certain animal has been eliminated, mainly by man without thinking, there has been more havoc created than could be imagined. In Texas there has been the elimination of the Mountain Lion, which more or less controlled the population of the deer. The results did not show up at first but in a few years the proponents for the killing of the Mountain Lions and sportsmen found, to their dismay, that many deer had starved to death because of food shortage. The increase of the herds had led to the overgrazing of the land.

A still more graphic picture of a tremendous increase of one kind of animal population, and what can happen when man thinks he is wiser than Mother Nature, occurred in Australia. In the 19th century, sportsmen decided to import hares from the U.S. to Australia, which it was hoped would provide small game for the hunter. There were no hares or rabbits on that continent before this. Within a very few years after this importation, the continent was fairly overrun by the hares. They invaded the cultivated land and caused immeasurable damage, until the farmers started a concentrated drive to eliminate the pest. What was the reason for this rapid increase? Australia has very few carnivorous predators and as rabbits are notoriously prolific there was no natural control to cut down the huge rabbit population. The above example has made man stop and think carefully about all the ecological factors involved when a decision to transplant flora or fauna out of its original habitat is considered.

MULE DEER *(Odocoileus hemionus)*

JB

All animals are not Lilliputian in the Elfin Forest. I have seen at least one or more herds of Mule Deer, browsing in the meadows and Chaparral at least once each winter when riding into back country.

The common name, Mule Deer sounds like this is an awkward beast, but the "mule" name comes from the size of the ears, and the deer is most graceful in all its actions. Once you have seen an adult buck or doe take off into the cover of brush and trees, you will never forget how it bounds away with graceful ease. Truly a sight to be seen!

In the early morning, drive along a quiet stretch of highway or roadway in the late spring or early summer at about an elevation of 2,500 to 3,500 feet and try to keep a sharp eye on the meadows. Before too long you should see a doe or two, usually with their new born dapple-colored fawns. Occasionally there may be an antlered buck off from the group. One of two things may happen. If you stop the car and stay in it, the does, and any bucks, should raise their heads, snap their large mule-like ears toward you and look for a moment, then unconcerned, return to their browsing. But if you leave the car and they spot you, they may suddenly bound off for the heavy brush or forest trees for better cover. The bucks, with their brace of antlers that are regrowing usually disappear first. The does follow a little slower, as though waiting for the fawns to catch up.

Usually, in spring the bucks head for the higher ground, while the does are alone below awaiting the birth of their fawns. The bucks continue on up to 4,000 to 6,000 feet elevation during the heat of summer, ahead of the slower browsing does and young.

About one-fourth of all the Mule Deer births are twins, and rarely they will bear triplets. The baby deer weigh only 6 to 7 pounds at birth. However, within about four weeks the little fellows are in the meadow browsing with their mothers.

Some interesting facts about the Mule Deer are that the adult will weigh 100 to 195 pounds. When they bound off, often they will cover as much as 20 feet in one jump, and will travel as fast as 35 miles an hour. However, they are seldom able to maintain this speed for more than a quarter of a mile. While browsing for food they will often include the twigs and leaves of the willow, scrub oak, ash, sagebrush, berry bushes, wild grape, plus fruit and mistletoe, when it can be reached, then top it all off with mushrooms! The head of the family herd, the senior buck, usually returns to his family and harem in early fall. He chases off the young bucks and takes over during the rutting season. After the rutting season is over all the bucks join the does on the feeding grounds.

JB   (b).

Mule Deer with (a) horns in velvet, (b) full set of mature horns, (c) type of tail.

Badger
Taxidea taxus
LM

JB
Striped Skunk
Mephitis mephitis

Gray Fox
Urocyon cinereoargenteus
LM

Coyote
Canis latrans
LM

Mountain Lion
Felis concolor
LM

Bobcat
LM *Lynx rufus*

Western Gray Squirrel *Sciuru griseus*
LM

Merriam Chipmunk
Eutamias merriami
JB

Cottontail
Sylvilagus audubonii
LM

Valley Pocket Gopher
Thomomys bottae
LM

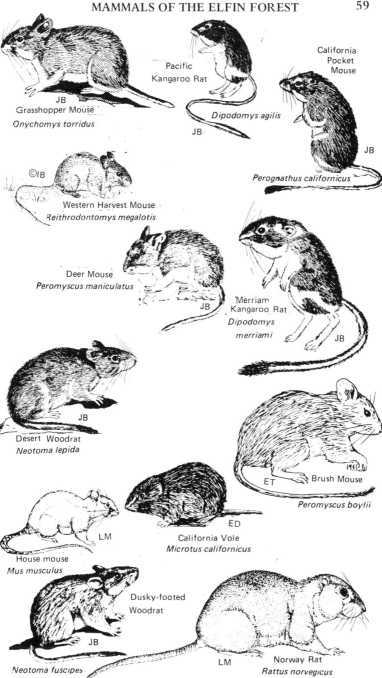

Pacific
Kangaroo Rat

JB
Grasshopper Mouse
Onychomys torridus

Dipodomys agilis
JB

California
Pocket
Mouse

JB

Perognathus californicus

©IB

Western Harvest Mouse
Reithrodontomys megalotis

Deer Mouse
Peromyscus maniculatus
JB

Merriam
Kangaroo Rat
*Dipodomys
merriami*
JB

Desert Woodrat
Neotoma lepida
JB

Brush Mouse
ET
Peromyscus boylii

House mouse
Mus musculus
LM

California Vole
Microtus californicus
ED

Dusky-footed
Woodrat
JB

Norway Rat
Rattus norvegicus
LM

Neotoma fuscipes

GMC
Turkey Vulture
(R)

JGI
Red-tailed
Hawk
(R)

JGI
Cooper's Hawk
(R)

JGI
Sharp-shinned
Hawk
(R&WV)

JB
Prairie
Falcon
(R)

JB
Sparrow Hawk
(R)

JB
(R*WV)
Band-tailed
Pigeon

JB
Mourning Dove
(SV&R)

CB
Golden Eagle
(R)

JGI
Barn Owl
(R)

JB
Screech Owl
(R)

©IB
Black-chinned
Hummingbird
(SV)

©IB
Vaux's
Swift
(SV)

JGI
Anna's ♀
Hummingbird
(R)

©IB
Rufous Hummingbird ♂
(Migrant)

JGI
Belted
Kingfisher
(R)

JB ♂
Allen's Hummingbird
(SV)

JGI

CHAPTER 9

BIRDS OF THE ELFIN FOREST

The study of birds is an engrossing subject. Many volumes have been written about birds. Artists have spent their life time painting them. Naturalists and students, kings and paupers, engineers and aerodynamatrists and children too have all been fascinated by the feathered creatures of the world. From east to west, pole to pole in one form or another birds are just about everywhere. Some weigh an ounce or two, and others tip the scale at over 100 pounds. Some can fly well over 25,000 miles a year, while others have never flown. Some live in water and others live on land. What I shall write about birds of the Elfin Forest is hardly a scratch on the surface of the potential possible study awaiting an interested person.

One of the most interesting hobbies and one that many people pursue, is that of bird watching and identification. It is a simple hobby to get into, and requires no expensive equipment. A good guide book, a pair of center focusing and adjusting binoculars, a note book and pencil, and the real desire to learn by watching. Such a hobby sharpens a person's ability to observe details, for details really count for that final identification. Often this observation has to be accomplished in a matter of seconds, for a bird in good health is seldom still for long.

In those seconds you should note several key points that will assist considerably in the final identificaion.

1. Note the size of the bird, not in inches, but in comparative size with other known birds - such as "larger than a sparrow" or "smaller than a morning dove". Estimating inches at a distance of 10 yards is seldom accurate.
2. Note size, shape and color of the bill.
3. Note type, shape and use of feet.

If time permits, check the arrangement of the feather colors, (use the same color chart as that for wild flowers). Note special markings, such as "white bars on the wings" (white stripes). Check form, color,

*Scrub Jay *(Aphelocoma coerulescens)*

size and use of the tail. Finally, note surroundings where the observation was made—bushes, trees, bare ground, meadows or lawns. If possible, note what the bird is eating. Be sure to note the weather, temperature and date.

If at any time during the observation the bird starts to move about, such as hopping on the ground, like a sparrow, or walks like a blackbird, make a note of that. Should it fly, note the flying action. Do the wings beat constantly; does it soar; or does it beat its wings for a moment and then soar? All of these minute notes will come in handy when you have a chance to sit down with your guide book and make a study of the bird. Never be afraid of making too many notes regardless how insignificant they may seem. The more the better. Do not trust your memory; all too often what you think will be remembered is forgotten within a few hours; that could well be the one key clue to the entire identification.

One item that can be of immeasurable assistance to the amateur, is a local bird-list. Usually these are available at a local museum of natural history or zoo, or college bookstore. These lists may consist of one or more mimeographed pages or in the form of a pamphlet. Most of these lists are free of charge, but if there is a charge, it is usually nominal for the information it contains. With such a list at hand much searching for a bird that simply does not exist in the area will be eliminated, unless you have run on to a drifter that has wandered off course and found a haven in your locale. Be sure to notify your local source where you obtained the list of birds. They may give you credit for the discovery, and make you feel a bit like Columbus.

Here are a few suggestions and precautions that may help you on a bird-walk or hike:

1. The best times to look for birds are in the early morning or early evening. In either case walk away from the sun. In the morning set your trail to the west and in the evenings to the east. If you walk towards the sun most of the birds become silhouettes.

2. Wear clothes that do not clash in color with your surroundings. Dark clothes (dark brown, green or blue) for dark surroundings and light colored clothes for light surroundings.

3. Wear your binoculars in the ready position, on a strap around your neck. Glasses should be focused for 15 to 25 feet.

4. Walk softly. Wear tennis shoes if you are to travel on a smooth trail or roadway. Do not carry a walking stick or cane.

5. If you are to be in a certain area for several days take along a little grain or bread crumbs. Spread them in a place you are likely to return to the following day. Do this several times and add a couple of containers of water. Before you know it, the birds will soon expect you at your own bird sanctuary.

6. Avoid taking the house pet along. Often a dog or cat, not satisfied with your idea of bird watching, wants a closer look!

7. Bird communities vary. In one locale there may be only Scrub Jays. A thousand feet away you may come upon a community of Black Birds. Set up several feeding stations in the areas that appeal to you. This same procedure is true in the city.

Don't feel that you are alone in the hobby of bird watching. It is estimated, that there are better than a million people engaged in the hobby in the United States.

MOST QUESTIONS ANSWERED THROUGH OBSERVATION

In most cases children have been the ones to ask me the unanswerable questions. But this puzzler was from an adult. A woman wrote and said that she had gone through several bird books trying to find out where all the birds went at night? That was a good question, and one that I had asked myself.

I started through my bird notebook. Sure enough, I came upon an entry which was titled "Bird Roosting". In my letter to the lady I quoted the following entry from the Note Book:

"June 10, 1960—5:30 AM—At Cabin (Potrero, Calif.)—sky clear— temperature 47° —no wind—walking east on dirt road." Usually in the pre-dawn I walked to the east from our cabin for about an hour, then as the sun came up I headed back, with the sun behind me, and the breeze in my face. "Heard birds in small Scrub Oak". As the eastern sky started to light up I heard a number of birds chattering in a small Scrub Oak Tree. "Attached marker, chattering stopped". I could not see the birds, so I attached a leaf from my notebook on a limb to mark it for a closer look upon my return. As I jiggled the branch a little the chattering stopped. They were aware that something was around their tree.

"Return, trunk straight, first branch 5 feet up." Upon my return I stopped to have that look. The tree trunk was straight, and free of branches for about five feet up. I wondered if this tree had been especially safe from snakes, animals and other natural enemies. "No birds; found droppings". There were no birds in the tree then. I climbed up on the first strong branch for a closer look and found one branch well concealed from the ground and rather well covered with droppings. A little below this branch I found still more droppings, which indicated that birds had perched there for a long time.

"Same night, 6 Sparrows, Junco, Scrub Jay". That night, I went back to have another look. The tree was still marked. I pointed my flashlight up into the tree, where I had been that morning. There was twittering, and the sound of beating wings. And sure enough I saw six Sparrows, a Mountain Junco, and of all things a Scrub Jay. I snapped off my light. After all I was invading the privacy of their bedroom. The one thing I did learn was, where these birds went at night, and the other was that they did not mind strange bed fellows.

This shows that through careful observation, much can be learned, and a few words in a notebook will preserve the information.

One of the first birds that you may encounter in the Elfin Forest, especially if you park or camp overnight in one of the many Live Oak groves, that have been designated as recreation areas, is the raucous voice of the Scrub Blue Jay *(Aphelocoma coerulescens)*. The Jay belongs to the same family as the crow and magpie and is the most conspicuous and noisy inhabitant of the Forest.

Some write that the Jay Bird is the "Dandy of the Crow family". This may be true of other Jays with brighter colored plumage, and even the Scrub Jay in more northerly California habitats, but certainly not our rather drab Southern California Scrub Jay. True, he sports a blue head, blue on the wings and tail. The back is usually gray to an olive drab. The breast is a dirty gray but with a small bib of black across the top of the breast. There is usually a small light line over each eye and he has a powerful black bill. He does not sport a crest, like his cousin, the Steller Jay to be found at higher elevations, and to the north of the Elfin Forest.

The Scrub Jay will usually greet you with a shrill "chey-chey-chey" or even "cheek-cheek-cheek", and at times a rasping "kwesh-kwesh-kwesh". All these sounds are like an air-raid alarm. The smaller birds take to their wings and head for a safer place, the squirrels heed the alarm and head for the burrows or the high branches of a tree. Truly he is the guardian of his community!

Even when you have stopped to set up camp, Mr. Jay keeps an eye on you. He will jump from limb to limb of the trees and bushes, often landing on the ground and hopping as close as he dares to watch you work. He is not too proud to accept a handout of bread crusts and crackers. But one warning—don't leave anything eatable on your picnic table and walk off and leave it. It won't be there when you return, and the Jays will be a little better fed than when you left. On one occasion we camped in a rather remote camp site. I took a large piece of canned ham, wrapped in a double layer of aluminum foil and put it upon the camp table. We were pitching the tent when I happened to glance at the table. Two large Scrub Jays were working on the ham like a woodpecker. They had pierced the foil and were feasting on the ham!

The Scrub Jay has a split personality. In the spring it will raid other bird nests, eat the eggs and the young, then tear the nest apart. On the other hand, in mating season the male has a very pleasing song that he sings "for her ears alone", and then he and his mate select the location of their nest with great care. Both the male and female work together in building their rather twiggy nest in a Scrub Oak, Blackberry bush, Poison Oak bush, or in a clump of Mistletoe, or any other Chaparral bush that suits them. The female will lay 3 to 6 reddish or greenish spotted eggs, and then she incubates them. Colors of the Srcub Jay's eggs are widely varied and beautiful. The male sometimes feeds her, but seldom sits on the eggs. During this time, both birds become most docile and quiet. However, if you or some animal approaches the nest area, the male becomes a fierce fighter, with nothing too big for him to challenge. I have seen a Scrub Jay attack a horse that approached too close to the nest. The horse retreated after the second attack.

On another camping trip when we decided to set up our tent in a fair sized oak grove, I noticed a number of young green acorns lying on the ground and they all appeared to have been neatly cut in half with a sharp pen knife. At first I thought it was the work of some human who had nothing better to do, but a further inspection of the ground under other trees found me several more. With my binoculars I could see several acorns similarly cut but still attached to the tree branch. My first thought was that this must have been done by squirrels. But then I realized that the acorns still on the tree were located at the ends of very small twigs that never could have supported a squirrel. Then came the answer. A Scrub Jay landed in the tree I was looking at. He worked himself around a twig until he faced the pointed end of an acorn. With a little maneuvering of his bill, then snip, the acorn was cut in half. The Jay then went to work on the inside of the nut with much gusto!

MOUNTAIN QUAIL *(Oreortyx pictus)*

In the grassy brush of the Chaparral belt, almost the year around, you will hear a call that will soon become very familiar "t-woook" or "ti-yoork". At other times it may sound like "wook" or "t-wook". It is the voice of the Mountain Quail, a cousin of the official bird of California, the California Quail.

The Mountain Quail is fairly easy to recognize. It is about the size of a dove, with a dark olive-brown color on its back, and the underside a chocolate and white mixed. Often it will be seen along the edge of bushes, like the rabbit, or seen following small trails in the weeds. It is distinguished from the California Quail by the long, straight, black, head plume on the male. The female has a shorter straight plume. The sides of the bird appear to be black, white, and chocolate barred. The bill is short and thick and usually appears to be black. Their diet consists mainly of berries, seeds, and insects.

The quail in this area travel in a small covey of about eight to ten adults. When they rest during the noon heat of the day, they form a circle with their heads facing out, and their tails together. If they are startled, the covey suddenly takes off in all directions, like an explosion. This action completely confuses the hunter as well as a predator. The same tactics are used when they settle down for the night.

The male has another cute maneuver. When the hen ventures out with her chicks from the hollowed out nest in the ground, the male will usually be with the family. If there is a threat of any sort, he will give a signal. The chicks immediately squat down in the weeds, as does the hen. The male will slowly and silently move away from the group. If the danger approaches closer, he suddenly takes to the air with a wild beating of his stubby wings and at the same time lets out a distracting whistling sound. He may fly low over the tops of the Chaparral for 300 to 500 feet, then plunge into the bush. This usually throws the enemy off the track, keeping the family safe.

The Mountain Quail is listed as a non-migratory bird. This is true except that they do migrate within the Elfin Forest. In the winter when temperatures often drop below freezing, they will make their way to lower levels, and return to higher places when summer starts.

This quail is a wise bird in many ways, but in others, it is rather stupid. They almost always make their nests in slight depressions in the earth, where the hen lays 12 to 15 eggs. I have heard hunters and hikers tell of how they have stepped flat footed into one of these nests and ruined the entire clutch of eggs.

All quail in the State of California are now protected by State Law; and for good reason. At the turn of the century, quail of several species were most prolific throughout the state. Hunters found it profitable to hunt them and sell them as a delicacy. There is on record, an account of two hunters delivering 300 dozen birds to a restaurant in two weeks time! Quail on toast sold for 30¢ a serving.

The California Indians would often set snares for the wild fowl to add to their meager diets. The modern hunters now have certain seasons and localities where they can hunt a set limit.

I heard a strange story from an old man who drove a dilapidated car from one public camp ground to another in order to save paying rent and be able to live on his very small pension. While talking to him, he invited me to stay for supper. He insisted so much that I finally agreed. He did ask me not to tell anyone about the main dish because it was to be roasted quail. I mentioned that they were out of season. He admitted that he knew that they were, so he had trapped them. I asked him how he had accomplished this feat. He explained that he would seek out a trail in the grass that the quail would frequent. There he would put a line of cracked corn with one kernel on the trap-trigger of a mouse trap. When the quail would hit the trigger, bop! a broken neck. So that's another weak point of the quail. They taste too good!

ROADRUNNER *(Geococcyx californianus)*

It wouldn't be fair not to mention this fabulous fellow and add his name to the list of birds that you are almost sure to see on your first visit to the Elfin Forest. True, you may not see one if you are on foot, but you can hardly miss a sight of one or more Roadrunners, if you are in an auto. Usually they will appear on the road as you round a sharp corner. There is little likelihood of running over this bird, for he will be off like the wind on his long, strong legs.

Surprisingly, the Roadrunner is a member of the cuckoo family. It is a rather large bird, 20 to 24 inches in length, with long black legs that leave a foot print showing two toes pointing ahead and two to the rear. This is known as zygodactyl shaped to the ornithologist (a person knowledgeable in the branch of zoology that deals with birds). The Roadrunner runs fast for his size, going 15 miles an hour or more.

When the covered wagon pioneers arrived in the Elfin Forest and they saw these strange birds, they called them "Chaparral Cocks". As these new settlers picked out their locations and built cabins, they would tame the Roadrunners to be pets and kept them in and around their homes. They were found to be excellent in catching rodents, lizards, snakes, and many insects. In those days the pioneers did not have the luxury of housecats.

The Roadrunners are slender, with brown-black and white heavily streaked sides and wings. Their undersides are white, but may appear a more buff color if they have recently been in a tussle with a snake, or other small animal that makes up the Roadrunner's diet. He sports a shaggy, speckled, black and white crest on his head. There is a white narrow bar that runs from the top part of the bill to over the eye and to about half an inch beyond that where the bar ends with a red spot. The bill is shaped much like the woodpeckers, and will often be one and a half to two inches long, a blackish brown color. The legs are yellowish-gray while young. When he flies, which is not often, the rather short rounded wings will show a white crescent below.

For a bird of his size and habit, he has a strange voice, singing six to eight dove-like coos in a descending pitch with the last coo on about the same pitch as a Mourning Dove. He sometimes will rattle his mandibles together and make a sound something like "br-r-r".

The male and female Roadrunner are just about the same in appearance. The nest is usually a shallow shaped affair located in low bushes and trees and even in cactus clumps! The bird can enter the nest on foot as well as on the wing. After they mate, 3 to 8 white eggs are laid. The eggs are brooded, counting when the first egg is laid, so that the chicks will hatch one at a time.

I once almost had the chance to see a fight, which I am sure would have been to the death, between a Roadrunner and a Rattlesnake, 2½ to 3 feet long. The two were in a clearing just off the narrow paved road. The snake was coiled with his head raised as though ready to strike. The Roadrunner was circling the reptile slowly, then he would fan out his tail feathers and slightly flutter his stubby wings. I pulled my car up by the side of the roadway and took out my field glasses to better see this battle. The bird would slowly circle the snake until the snake would have to unwind its head. Their eyes seemed to be locked to one another. While the snake's head was turned away the bird would try a grab for it with his bill. But the snake was too fast, and the bird would then start the same tactics in the opposite direction. It was obvious that the Roadrunner had the best of the snake. I felt that the battle would last about ten minutes more and that the bird would be the winner. At about this time a car came up rapidly behind me. There was a loud tooting of the horn, and then he passed me and the place where the battle was in progress. When the dust had cleared away, both Roadrunner and snake were gone. The loud horn or the rushing car had scared off the protagonists.

Rather disappointed, I started up my car and slowly passed the place of battle. I could not see any sign of snake or bird. However, I did see a small blotch of what appeared to be blood in the dust. It could have been oil. Because of the oncoming traffic I went on my way.

Incidentally, the Roadrunner is New Mexico's official State Bird.

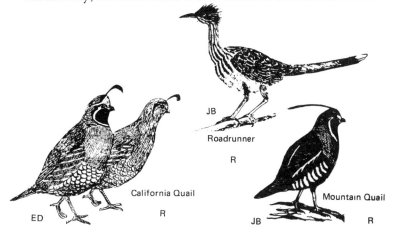

JB
Roadrunner
R

California Quail
ED   R

Mountain Quail
JB   R

Red-shafted Flicker (R)

Nuttall's Woodpecker (R)

Hairy Woodpecker (R)

Acorn Woodpecker (R)

Downy Woodpecker (R)

Western Kingbird (SV)

Cassin's Kingbird (Partly R)

Western Wood Pewee (SV)

Say's Phoebe (Partly R)

Black Phoebe

Tree Swallow (Partly R)

Violet-green Swallow (SV)

Horned Lark (R)

Cliff Swallow (SV)

Barn Swallow (SV)

Yellow-billed Magpie (R)

Key to Symbols of Bird Illustrations: R—Resident; SV—Summer Visitor; WV—Winter Visitor; †—Unprotected birds; *—Protected bird with certain open hunting seasons.

Crow
(R)
JB

Chestnut-backed
Chickadee
(R)
JB

Plain
Titmouse
(R)

House Wren
(SV)
JB
JGI

Wren-tit
(R)
JB

Long-billed
Marsh Wren
(R)
JB

White-breasted
Nuthatch
(R)
JB

Bush-tit
(R)
JB

Rock Wren
(R)
JB

Bewick's
Wren
(R)
JB

Mockingbird
(R)
JB

Cañon Wren
(R)
JB

California Thrasher
(R)
JB

JB
Robin
(WV&R)

JB
Varied Thrush
(WV)

JB
Mountain Bluebird
(Mostly WV)

JB
Swainson's Thrush
(SV)

Hermit Thrush
(SV&WV)
JB

Western Bluebird (R)
JB

(R)
Golden-crowned
Kinglet

ED

Ruby-crowned Kinglet
(R&WV)
ED

Cedar Waxwing
(Mostly WV)
JGI

JB
Water Pipit
(WV)

JB
Phainopepla
(R)

JB
Hutton's Vireo
(R)

JB
Loggerhead Shrike
(R)

Myrtle Warbler
(WV)

Orange-crowned Warbler
(SV&R)

Yellow Warbler
(SV)

(R)
Yellowthroat

Wilson's Warbler
(SV)

Audubon's Warbler
(SV&WV)

Townsend's Warbler
(WV)

©IB

English Sparrow
(R)

(R)
Western Meadowlark

Brewer's Blackbird   (R)

Red-winged Blackbird
(R)

Brown-headed Cowbird
(R)

Western Tanager
(SV&migrant)

Hooded Oriole
(Mostly SV)

Bullock's Oriole
(SV)

Black-headed
Grosbeak
(SV)

(SV)

Lazuli Bunting

JB

JB

Purple Finch
(R&WV)

JB

Lesser Goldfinch
(R)

JB

House Finch
(R)

JGI

American Goldfinch
(R)

JB

Brown Towhee
(R)

JGI

Savannah Sparrow
(R&WV)

JB

Lark Sparrow
(R)

P&GM

Oregon Junco
(R&WV)

JB

Chipping
Sparrow
(Mostly SV)

JB

Golden-crowned
Sparrow
(WV)

JB

JB

White-crowned
Sparrow (WV)

JB

Fox Sparrow
(WV&R)

©IB

Song Sparrow
R

CHAPTER 10

REPTILES OF THE ELFIN FOREST

A strange phenomenon among humans, is that some of us feel an extreme terror about certain things, harmless or otherwise. While in the service, I once knew a very brave man who would stand up against any enemy. I had seen him perform against the enemy many times with little regard for the opposition gun fire. But if a bee, hornet or wasp came into the room, he would panic and almost faint with fright. I knew another huge hulk of a man who had a desperate fear of reptiles. When I showed him a color photograph of a snake he shuddered in absolute horror.

With this in mind, never try to frighten another person with the creatures of nature. It will only increase their fear and dread, and may cost you a good friend. This is especially true of children. Be considerate of them and in time they may overcome this excess of fear. Snakes are a good example of feared creatures and I shall tell a little about them in this chapter.

The Elfin Forest has only one really dangerous poisonous reptile, the Rattler. There are, however, a few small and rather rare snakes with rear of the mouth fangs, who can inflict a bite that is mildly poisonous. Usually these little fellows will not bite, however, unless they are roughly handled. That is their only protection, so don't hold this against them.

When planning an excursion where reptiles are likely to be found be wary of the Rattler. If it possibly can be done, read the latest and most reliable first aid manual, usually available at your nearest Red Cross office. Otherwise, here are a few elementary suggestions which I feel are good, for I have used them twice with success. (1) Always carry a snake bite kit, usually available at any good drug store. (2) Keep the victim quiet. (3) If the wound appears as two punctures in the skin, assume it is the bite of a Rattler. Apply a tourniquet between the wound and the heart. Tighten for fifteen minutes. Loosen for a few minutes. Repeat. If there are others in the party,

* Western Rattlesnake *(Crotalus viridis)*

have them locate the snake and identify it. If it is a Rattler bite, proceed as follows: (4) Make a small incision in the skin from one fang puncture to the other, approximately one eighth inch deep with a sharp instrument (razor blade, pen knife blade, or other). Sterilize it with a lighted match. Always make these cuts lengthwise along the arm or leg, never crosswise, as you may cut a vein. (5) Apply the suction cup of your snake bite kit if available. Otherwise apply your lips and suck the blood and poison from the wound. Spit it out, and continue for about half an hour. (6) Call a doctor or get the victim to one as soon as possible.

Fatal snake bites are rare in the United States. Less than 150 persons a year succumb to such accidents. It is a good idea to follow these few simple rules while in snake country, and most of the Elfin Forest may be considered snake country:

1. Wear boots with 8 inch high tops or leggings.
2. Stay clear of logs and rock piles.
3. Keep on well traveled trails and roadways.
4. Look sharply where you put your hands and feet when climbing.

Non-poisonous snake bites will usually appear as a "U" shaped pattern of teeth marks. At times these bites can be very painful, as their teeth usually are curved backwards to better hold their prey. Their bite may hang up, causing a ripping wound to the skin. In most cases the wound can be treated as a regular puncture wound with a good germicide and protected with a bandage. In any case it is wise to hurry the victim to a doctor as soon as possible.

A few fables have persisted through the years about reptiles. The tale about the Hoop Snake actually a Mud Snake found mostly in southeastern United States, that supposedly grasps its tail in its mouth and then rolls like a hoop down the road is not based on fact. The same tale is told about the Western Racer, which is equally false. Some have said that a snake has a hypnotic power, mainly over birds. See the story in Chapter Nine about the Roadrunner and the Rattler. From that account it seems to be just the other way around! How many times have you heard that toads cause warts? Again this is not based on fact. Some species DO exude a substance that has a disagreeable odor and may cause a skin irritation. This substance is a form of protection from the toad's natural enemies.

Some lizards do lose their tails when seized by this appendage, which is especially adapted for shedding and will grow another one.

This is just another ruse to evade its enemies. The Horned Toad (actually a lizard) will squirt a harmless stream of blood from the forward corner of the eyes when first captured. This is another of the many tricks used by wild creatures to protect themselves from enemies.

In most cases the male and female snake look alike. Only a very few species will show a difference in color and pattern. The male will be somewhat smaller and have a longer tail while the female will have a longer body. Identification in snakes is made by the arrangement and number of their scales. See the suggested references at the back of the book for help in identification.

The snakes will feed on the living animals of the Elfin Forest. Some snakes exist mostly on eggs. In many cases snakes will swallow their food whole by the rearrangement of the flexible jaws which have two elongate moveable parts, the quadrate and supratemporal. Some snakes regurgitate eggshells, etc., after the contents have been swallowed, others swallow their food whole, and digest it all within the body cavity. Some snakes will crush or suffocate their victims and still others depend upon the poisonous venom to aid them.

Snakes do not have good vision but they are very alert to the slightest movement. Some snakes (pit vipers) can locate their victims by their body heat. These snakes have heat sensory organs or pits between the eye and nostril. Many snakes depend upon scent which is detectable through their tongue. The moist forked tip picks up and carries adherent odorous particles to a chamber (Jacobson's Organs) where sensory cells connect with the olfactory (smelling) lobes. Sluggish snakes depend almost entirely on the tongue method of detection. Experiments with water snakes have been made where their body has been smeared with an odorous secretion of frogs and fish and they tried to swallow their own selves!

These reptiles shed their outer skin once a year or as many as three times depending upon the species as well as if one is injured. The size of the snake has very little to do with the amount of times the snake sheds, but the shedding of the skin does allow the new underskin to expand and the snake increases in size. The skin will usually be turned back at the tip of the snout and rubbed off against rocks and other objects. The cast off skin is generally in-side-out.

It should be mentioned here, that there are movements starting in California for the preservation of reptiles and amphibians in the Elfin Forest and other locales. The needless killing of these creatures through fear and misunderstanding is upsetting the balance of Nature, and is costing the rancher and farmer more dollars every year. Rodent damage is appearing more often in grain storage for lack of control of the rodents. It is agreed that poisonous snakes should be disposed of around populated or habitated areas. But the harmless boa and gopher snake, etc., should be recognized and protected.

Just the other day, while I was working at my desk, I heard a commotion down the canyon. I could hear the excited voices of boys. I went to have a look. I found four lads, whom I knew slightly, standing around the pitiful remains of a badly mutilated Gopher Snake.

"What goes on, fellows?" I asked.

"We just killed a snake!" one boy jubilantly replied.

"But, Jim", I queried, "Why did you kill this one?"

"We-ll-ll, it's a snake, ain't it?" He replied slowly.

"Yes, Jim ", I replied, "it is a snake. A small Gopher Snake. It would have done very little if any damage to your ranch. Most of the things it would have done would have been of benefit to you and your Dad. It could have killed gophers, rats, and mice, better than any dog, cat or trap."

I invited the boys up to my cabin to show them colored photographs of the gopher and boa snakes, and a few words about their habits. Jim then told me that I should talk to his father, for it was he who had told him, to never trust a snake, and to kill them all.

The following week, I visited Jim's father. I found that he did not know anything about snakes. As a matter of fact, he had some sort of innate horror for anything that crawled. He admitted he was city born and raised and that the ranch, horses, and cattle were simply a form of recreation he had craved since his boyhood. He seemed happy to learn about snakes and amphibians. I am sure that the snakes, the boys, and I are just a bit more happy in our canyon.

The continued study of reptiles and amphibians is a most fascinating subject, in any Elfin Forest. It can be considered as a link in the chain of life from 120 million years ago up to today. The amateur's imagination can run rampant through the various transitions of the past. The amphibian's transition to the reptile, and the reptile's to the bird. Much thinking has already revealed fanciful theory in fact and fiction. Such a hobby could well lead to a full time profession and a lifetime of research. A dedicated study in the natural science field is certainly not over crowded.

RACERS

In the Elfin Forest there are two predominant species, the Striped Racer and the Western Red Racer. The Striped Racer (*Masticophis lateralis*) is easily recognized. It is usually 2 to 5 feet long, with grayish brown color above and a lighter tail, with a single pale yellowish stripe on each side. The Western Red Racer or Whipsnake (*Masticophis flagellum piceus*) grows somewhat longer, and is yellow to reddish brown in color. It has black cross-bands on the neck. It is often seen in the branches of a bush. Both are non-poisonous and beneficial. Both can climb in bushes after birds.

COMMON KINGSNAKE
(Lampropeltis getulus)
This has alternating rings of plain black or dark brown color with white. Sometimes it is striped, with a continuous pale yellow vertebral stripe. It it non-poisonous and beneficial. It may eat other snakes and lizards.

GOPHER SNAKE
(Pituophis melanoleucus catenifer)
This is perhaps the most common snake seen in the Elfin Forest. I have observed them from 2 feet to 8 feet long. Their colors can vary considerably. The most common colors are dark brown or nearly black blotches on a yellow-brown background. Usually the blotches are more widely spaced on the tail than on the body. It is believed that the Gopher Snake is strictly a daylight hunter, and I have never seen one in the open after the sun has set. It is non-poisonous and beneficial, but may be mistaken for a rattlesnake because of colors and a habit of rattling its tail in dry leaves.

RATTLESNAKES—
RED DIAMOND   AND WESTERN
Naturally, on both snakes rattles can be seen and heard. Both have wide arrow-shaped heads. On the Western Rattlesnake (*Crotalus viridis*), look for an olive green background with dark brown or black irregular blotches, bounded by a lighter color. A light stripe appears behind the eye. It is 2 to 6 feet long. The Red Diamond Rattlesnake (*Crotalus ruber*) is 2 to 5 feet long, and usually a shade of pink or red with diamond markings in dark brown; black and white rings are on the tail.

CALIFORNIA BOA

I have seen many Boas on our paved highways, both day and night in cold weather. They apparently are there to get warm from any heat radiating from the paving. Many small creatures of the Elfin Forest seek the paved highways. The California Boa (*Charina bottae*) is 2 to 3 feet long; thick bodied; and a red-brown color on a blueish background. This is sometimes called the two-headed snake because the tail is shaped like the head. It is non-poisonous and beneficial.

ALWAYS REMEMBER, MOST REPTILES WILL BITE if handled roughly. Although the bite may not be poisonous, due to the arrangement of their teeth, and the food some eat, they can inflict nasty wounds, prone to infection.

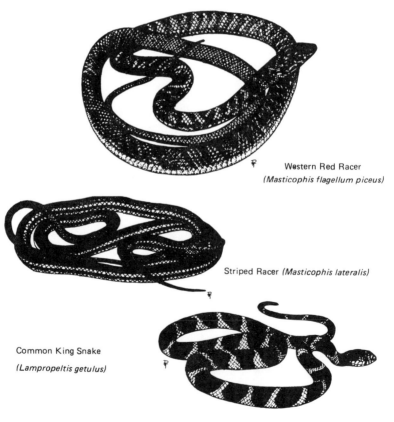

Western Red Racer
(*Masticophis flagellum piceus*)

Striped Racer (*Masticophis lateralis*)

Common King Snake
(*Lampropeltis getulus*)

Gopher Snake
(Pituophis melanoleucus catenifer)

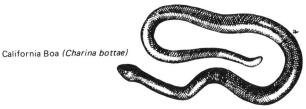

California Boa *(Charina bottae)*

LIZARDS COMMON TO THE ELFIN FOREST

California Legless Lizard *(Anniella pulchra)*

Western Banded Gecko *(Coleonyx variegatus)*

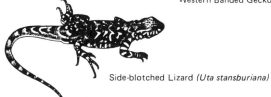

Side-blotched Lizard *(Uta stansburiana)*

Coast Horned Toad or Lizard
(Phrynosoma coronatum)

Western Fence Lizard
(Sceloporus occidentalis)

Granite Spiny Lizard
(Sceloporus orcutti)

Granite Night Lizard
(Xantusia henshawi)

Western Skink
(Eumeces skiltonianus)

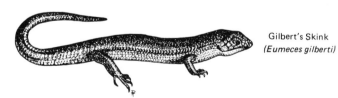

Gilbert's Skink
(Eumeces gilberti)

cut a carton top on only three sides, when unpacking one for his shelves. This could leave an excellent cover for the box to keep out sun and dirt, and make for neater packing in the automobile.

After our return from a camping trip, all the plastic bottles are emptied, the tops loosely screwed on, and the bottles replaced in the cartons. A few days before leaving on another trip, a teaspoonful of plain soda is put into each bottle, with about two cups of fresh water. This is shaken up well and the liquid is then discarded. When the bottles are refilled, the water is clean, sweet, and fresh.

Another item helpful in transporting water is a large (about five gallon capacity) plastic trash basket, with a snap-on cover. This is filled with various supplies while on our trip out. At the campsite we unpack the basket and put all the used water in it. This gives an excellent supply of otherwise worthless water for dousing the campfire. This of course is an additional boon due to the scarcity of water and fire hazardous conditions in a really dry camp

EMERGENCY FOOD SUPPLY

It may not seem necessary, but on several occasions we have been happy to have had our little emergency food supply. On one trip to the Chaparral, in the middle of April, some years ago, this food supply proved its worth. As my companions and I came over the crest of the mountains on the road home, we were suddenly confronted with a heavy snow storm. We knew we were in trouble before we had traveled three miles through the valley below. In that time, the snow had dropped nearly a foot on the road. We stopped for gas. That was our first delay, but we were low after the desert trip. Next it was decided that chains were in order for the car. More delay, and meanwhile the snowfall had increased. As we started up the next grade, we knew we were in real trouble. We could not make it through the mass of snow, AND the skidding cars.

Returning to the valley we found that the hotel and motels were more than filled. There simply was no place to bed down five more; plus that, finances were at an all time low! We ended up in a very small camping area that we had known in the summertime. With difficulty, we managed to erect our cumbersome tent under a large clump of Scrub Oak. Next I managed to set up my faithful (10 year old) Coleman stove in the tent, along with a single mantle lamp.

CHAPTER 11

CAMPING IN THE ELFIN FOREST

It is not the intention to tell anyone how to camp; any family or individual who is interested in the outdoors has their own set ways. But because there are a great many people who have migrated from other parts of our great country into California and because in camping these places often had different conveniences and accommodations than we have in the Elfin Forest, a few tips may prove helpful, and make this fascinating country more hospitable to all.

WATER

One of the first lessons it is important to learn, is to consider all southern State and Federal campsites as "Dry", regardless of what the road maps and camp guides might say or indicate. True, there may be some water at your destination, but often the taste is strange and at times almost unpalatable, (especially to children). The chemical content can often cause upset stomachs. Water that is available from filling station hoses can be equally offensive to the taste.

Water from streams and lakes, should be looked at with extreme caution. Not because of the water itself, but the possible contamination from the hands and habits of other campers. Many campers are careful, but some do not think of others who come after them or the other fellow down stream. If you must take your water from such sources, be sure to boil it for about ten minutes. It won't hurt the water, and it will make it a lot healthier to drink.

Our solution to this problem was rather simple, and at no cost to us. We gathered up a dozen empty plastic bleach and starch bottles. These were thoroughly cleaned. The small piece of sealing paper in the screw-on tops was replaced with sealers of our own manufacturing. A bit of negotiation with the local grocer produced sturdy cardboard cartons, with cardboard dividers, for ease in transporting them in our station wagon. Even better, you might try and have the grocer

Both were filled with fuel. I set the stove oven in place over the flame, and by darkness, we were snug and fairly warm after a steaming cup of chocolate. During the war, I had sworn that I would never eat a meal of Spam and beans again, but that night I ate them with the gusto I would usually give a steak. The same applied to the dried eggs and spam the next morning. Both dinner and breakfast were more than adequate. So, if I had not had that emergency kit tucked away in the camping gear, I don't exactly know what would have happened. The next morning we learned from the Highway Patrolman that the oil supply for the hotel and motel had been exhausted during the night, and that the occupants had had a rough night, while between our car heater and the Coleman stove in the tent we had fared very well. The road was cleared by ten that morning, and we all returned home happy, to the relief of friends and relations, a day late, true, but bless those supplies!

Other times we have used that little box of canned goods when we have had car trouble; during forest fires; and because of auto wrecks.

What to put in such a kit? Let your preferences be your guide. We pack baked beans, canned meats, canned soups, canned breads (Boston brown bread has been our favorite), canned fruits or sauces. Also we put in small individual foil-wrapped envelopes of chocolate, packaged teabags (re-wrapped in aluminum foil) and a small unbreakable container of coffee. All supplies are dated on the day they are put into the kit, and replaced every two years. Each spring, the kit is opened for inspection to be ready for the new camping season. As I recall, the only spoilage we have had was with a can of foreign made bacon. For bread, we have tried packaged biscuit mix re-wrapped with foil, but have found after about 8-10 months that it does become rancid.

REFRIGERATION WHILE CAMPING

It is too bad that so many people still have the habit of dumping a solid piece of ice into their camp ice chest compartment, popping their food into the compartment at kitchen temperatures, clamping the lid down and heading for the hills without a worry. When they arrive at their camp or picnic grounds, the chest is opened, and oh boy! What a mess! In those hours they have been on the road, plus the fact that the ice was put in a warm chest, there is usually several inches of water in the bottom that has been sloshed around for the past 50 miles. The meat is soggy and tasteless from the soaking, the hamburger patties are full of water, and the potato salad - ugh!

We have had this happen to us a couple of times, until we came up with this simple solution:

1. Several half gallon milk cartons were filled with tap water and placed in the freezer.
2. Several quart size milk cartons were filled with various flavored non-carbonated fruit drinks, that were already sweetened and ready for use. These were also placed in the freezer. Be sure to mark them accordingly.
3. A half gallon carton of iced tea was put in the freezer.
4. Milk was put into the freezer also according to expected needs.
5. Home made soup frozen ahead of time in milk cartons, and used when needed is excellent fare. Also stew and bean dishes.

The night before our expected departure, the ice cube trays were emptied into the ice chest along with an opened carton of the frozen water. The lid was clamped into place on the chest, and left to chill overnight. All foods that were expected to go along with us were prepared the day before, then thoroughly chilled in the refrigerator. The next morning the chest was emptied, dried hurriedly, then the ice chest compartment was re-packed with the cartons of frozen liquids and other frozen and chilled foods, in approximately the order they were expected to be used.

By using this simple method, protecting the chest from the direct rays of the sun, usually covered in the rear of the car, opening it only when necessary and for the shortest possible time, we have maintained fair refrigeration for as many as four days. Most vegetables and fruits do well in a loose woven cloth or burlap sack hung by a rope in the open air, with an occasional half cup of water poured over them from the top. Try to purchase vegetables as fresh as possible, and leave their tops on. There is usually plenty of good water stored in those leafy tops.

Never fail to take advantage of the running streams for refrigeration. Closed or tightly covered containers placed in the running streams stay remarkably cool. Be sure and ANCHOR them to shore, for they have a most unusual way of mysteriously disappearing.

INSECTS

Insects have a way of making a camping trip a miserable experience. Yellow Jackets have an annoying way of trying to get your steak before you do. Flies can become troublesome around meal time. By accident, we found that by going up-wind or into the breeze about ten feet from the table, a couple of minutes before the food is set there, and spraying a small quantity of insect repellent, preferably botanical compounds, with a hand spray gun so that the spray drifts over the table, that this will usually provide a cleared, insect-free eating place for about 15 to 20 minutes.

PERSONAL CLEANLINESS IN CAMP

Should rest rooms not be available, or too distant from the camp, it is a simple task to improvise one. Set it up down-wind from the campsite , in a secluded spot, protected by canvas or other suitable material (blanket, etc.) for privacy. Don't forget the tissue!!! It is amazing how important an item it can be, if forgotten.

An 18 to 24 inch deep trench, with a rest bar will usually suffice nicely. Be sure to cover it well before leaving camp.

Check a Boy Scout Handbook for many excellent suggestions which will make a camp a wonderful and healthful place to live, and to study one of our most valuable American Heritages, "nature".

THE CAMP FIRE

A camp without a campfire, just isn't a camp.

The first thing one must learn in California is that regardless of what kind of fuel and container you plan to use: gasoline stove, butane gas, kerosene, or a wood fire in the camp stoves, usually provided, you must have a fire permit. These permits are free and are issued by most any member of the California Forestry Department. I procured my recent permit from a member of a trash collecting crew of the department. These permits are also available from the Ranger Stations.

If you intend to use the efficient wood stoves provided at regular camp grounds, don't depend upon finding or gathering wood in the brush around the area. Consider that the camping area has been in use for a number of years, and those before you have pretty well cleaned out all the dead wood. We have found it much more efficient and less bothersome to take along a bundle of pressed logs found in many markets. A small hand axe or hatchet is just right for chipping off what fuel is needed. We also have found that the regular liquid charcoal starter is excellent as a fire starter. Soak three or four chips well, with it and place them in the middle of other chips and light them with a match. However, NEVER ATTEMPT TO SQUIRT MORE FLUID ON A FIRE WHILE THERE ARE FLAMES OR COALS. There have been several fatal accidents when the sides of the can of lighter fluid have been released to permit more air into the can, and have apparently sucked the flame into direct contact with the inner contents and caused a terrific explosion.

Sticks that appear like wood, impregnated with an inflammable substance which easily take the flame of a match, in wet or dry weather, and burn without fumes, smoke, or sparks can be purchased. They come in log forms that are cut in lengths to fit an average home fireplace. These also work fine for starting the wood fire. As far as we have been able to learn from actual use, these logs are the safest fire starter of all we have tried.

If you are a family or individual who enjoys sitting around the campfire late into the evening, as we are, be sure to include a few fireplace size Oak logs. They burn without sparks and very little smoke and still have a most pleasant aroma. They will also burn with a low flame or coal for considerable time. We have an arrangement with a wood yard operator to purchase split Oak logs at his yard by the piece. A dollar's worth has proven plenty for a long weekend. Markets stock boxed oak logs. These logs are cut out of very good wood, which is neat to handle, and easy to pack in the car or trailer, but a bit more expensive.

PORTABLE RADIO

In these modern days of so many conveniences, we have developed the habit of carrying along a transister radio on our camping trips. You will find that it is not only a wonderful source of entertainment when time sometimes lags in conversation and things to do, but you can keep up with the world news. This may not seem important at first, but if you do not have a radio on the trip, about the first thing you will grab upon getting home is the stack of newspapers that have accumulated. There will be ball scores, politics, etc., you suddenly feel you have missed.

As a more experienced camper, I believe that the weather reports, road conditions in the area, and possible forest fires and their progress have been most important. On several trips that radio has saved us many miles of useless driving.

HUNTING AND GUNS

Personally, I am against any type of firearms on a family camping trip. Accidental wounding of loved ones, is all too common. Many of these accidents happen from lack of knowledge of the weapon or just plain carelessness. I do, however, believe in the gun for protection. The right to bear arms is still a part of our "Bill of Rights". However remember!!

If you should carry a firearm on these trips, and you suddenly get the urge to unlimber it and take a pot shot at a bunny or bird, RE-MEMBER that Game Preserves are not too well defined in the brush, and you may be in violation of the law. It is also well to remember that in many of these preserves it is a violation to even have an assembled firearm in your possession. Play real safe, check all the pros and cons of the gun problem well ahead of time.

CAMERA AND FILMS

It is always nice to have a picture record of the trip. If you can afford it, take the camera and plenty of film. You will cherish pictures of the family at play and at rest. Try for some good pictures of the natural flora and fauna. You will remember the areas better later and have many more good topics for study and conversation.

TOOLS

The tools that you normally carry in your car will usually fulfill your needs. About the only additional tools which I have found handy are a small hatchet, for splitting up the pressed logs and driving tent stakes. A small box of mixed nails and staples can be very handy. Recently I have found that a slightly heavy-headed hammer has been helpful in driving steel tent stakes into decomposed granite and has speeded things up a bit.

A FINAL WORD

The idea of going into the Elfin Forest, or any other similar place and playing like an Indian or rugged pioneer, is out as far as I am concerned. I feel, that if those staunch souls had what we have, they would have welcomed much of it. I believe that the modern camper should make his camp as comfortable and convenient as possible.

When you go camping today, go to enjoy yourself; to rest; and to enjoy what civilization has left for us. Live as you do at home, as far as possible. That's the way the pioneers and Indians did. So why not us?

Photographed by W. S. Head

CHAPTER 12

JB

*

CONSERVING NATURAL BEAUTY

Conservation in camping may seem rather an odd thing to bring up about small campsites . I shall try to bring up a few subjects that may be put into practice in camp that will help in a small way to conserve our precious wild life and recreational lands.

The best place to set up the practice of conservation is right in your camp. To begin with, make it a point to keep the site clean. Burn all unwanted papers, containers, etc. Burn all burnable garbage. Too often, people believe that such materials will be disposed of by the small animals and birds. This is not always true. Many wild creatures are very cautious about campsites where humans have been. They actually avoid such places. Food scraps that are left, in good faith, by campers will lay, attract flies, and simply rot. If you can't burn it, bury it deep, and leave a neat camp for the next fellow. How often I have pulled into camp and found it littered with various bits of refuse with the camp stove jammed with tin cans, bottles, and garbage, I would hate to say. My opinion of other campers would dip to an all time low.

Empty tin cans, bottles, and jars should never be discarded recklessly into the bushes or any other place, as a matter of fact. The cans should be rinsed with water, if possible, and the glass containers left capped or broken to bits in a safe place, preferably in the trash cans provided. Tin cans should be flattened on the open end before discarding. All this is suggested, because it may come as a surprise to you, but many thousands of small animals lose their lives, rather cruelly, when they get their little heads caught in them while trying to get at the remains.

Trees and bushes are the mainstay of the Elfin Forest, and they should be protected to the best of our ability. Never build a fire at the base of a tree; this can kill it. The deadly axe and knife are a real enemy. Adults, children, and lovers for some ungodly reason, like to leave their initials carved into the tree bark. It means nothing to any

* Rufous-sided Towhee, *Pipilo erythrophthalmus*

one else but to those who do this, and not only leaves unsightly marks, but provides an opening for boring insects, that could well cause the death of the tree or bush. Caution should be applied also when it does become necessary to drive a nail into a tree. It is an easy way for the insects to enter the tree. Always pull out a nail and then fill the hole with a plain wooden plug.

If you should come upon a seedling while tramping around through the brush, drive a small stake in the ground beside it, about four inches from the main stem, and you may protect the little fellow from the steps of another.

Be wary of picking wild flowers. When this great Southwest has had its proper amount of rain almost every hill, dale, and field will produce a bountiful crop of these natural jewels, and just like real jewels, they need your protection. If you must collect them, be wise and do it with a camera. Help to insure next years blooms.

If you have the time and inclination, check with the State Fish and Game Department or other state agencies for ways that you may help promote conservation. It can be an enjoyable voluntary task to become a part of the movement to preserve our wild life and lands.

BE GOOD TO THE OUT OF DOORS AND IT CAN BE GOOD TO YOU AND YOURS!!!

REFERENCES

Abrams, Leroy, *Illustrated Flora of the Pacific States*, Stanford University Press.

Bent, Arthur Cleveland, *Jays, Crows, and Titmice*, Smithsonian Institute, Washington, D. C.

Booth, Ernest Sheldon, *Birds of the West*, Stanford University Press.

Brown, Vinson, and George Lawrence, *The California Wildlife Region*, Naturegraph Publications.

Brown, Vinson, *How to Understand Animal Talk*, Little Brown and Company.

Brown, Vinson, Henry G. Weston Jr. *Handbook of California Birds*, Second revised edition, Naturegraph Publishers.

Burt, William H., Richard P. Grossenheider, *A Field Guide to the Mammals*, 2nd Edition, Houghton, Mifflin Company.

Ingles, Lloyd G., *Mammals of the Pacific States*, Stanford University Press.

Jaeger, Edmund C., *Desert Wild Flowers*, Stanford University Press.

Jepson, Willis Linn, *A Manual of Flowering Plants*, University of California Press.

Kirk, Donald R., *Wild Edible Plants*, Naturegraph Publishers.

Lutz, Frank E., *Field Book of Insects*, 3rd Edition, G. P. Putnam's Sons.

The Merck Veterinary Manual, 3rd edition, Merck & Company.

McKelvey, Susan Delano, *Botanical Exploration of the Trans-Mississippi West 1790-1850*, (Arboretum of Harvard University).

Montgomery, Rutherford G., *The Living Wilderness*, Dodd, Mead and Company.

Munz, Philip, *A California Flora*, University of California Press.

Peterson, Roger Tory, *A Field Guide to the Birds*, Houghton, Mifflin Company.

Seton, Ernest Thompson, *Lives of Game Animals*, Volume 4 Part II Charles T. Branford Company.

Stebbins, Robert C., *A Field Guide to Western Amphibians and Reptiles*, Houghton, Mifflin Company.

Swain, Ralph B., Ph. D., *The Insect Guide*, Doubleday and Company Inc.

Taylor, Norman, *Taylor's Encyclopedia of Gardening*, Houghton Mifflin Company.

ACKNOWLEDGEMENTS

I wish to acknowledge my appreciation of help from the following sources during my research days on the Elfin Forest. The El Cajon Library where I spent many hours. The Botanical Society of Balboa Park. The Museum of Natural History of Balboa Park where I obtained generous help from Dr. Linsey. Dr. Frank Gander, photographer and botanical curator who gave me good advice and inspiration to keep going on this book. And my very hard working and helpful wife. Others that were helpful with information were the California Department of Fish and Game, The Santa Rosa Memorial Library and the Rancho Santa Ana Botanic Garden, Claremont. The help of the following artists is appreciated also. Ron Goldman (RG), and Emily Reid, (ER) doing most of the plants, Jerry Buzzel (JB), most of the birds and mammals, Phyllis Thompson, (PT), Reptiles. Other illustrators are Lynn Maxwell (LM), Iain Baxter (©IB), Elizabeth Dasmann (ED), Virginia Cleveland (VC), Emily Thompson (ET), James Gordon Irving (JGI), Gene M. Christman (GMC), Clyde Burns (CB), Patricia and George Mattson (P&GM), and Sara Thompson, insect and insect galls.

INDEX   .* Indicates Illustrations